The Unofficial Strawberry Shortcake Cookbook

From Blueberry's Berry Versatile Muffins to Orange Blossom Layer Cake, 75 Recipes from the World of Strawberry Shortcake!

A.K. Whitney

This book is unofficial and unauthorized. It has not been approved, licensed, or endorsed by WildBrain Ltd., its affiliates, or any of its licensees.

ADAMS MEDIA

NEW YORK   LONDON   TORONTO   SYDNEY   NEW DELHI

Adams Media
An Imprint of Simon & Schuster, Inc.
100 Technology Center Drive
Stoughton, Massachusetts 02072

First Adams Media hardcover edition December 2022

For information about special discounts for bulk purchases, please contact Simon & Schuster Special Sales at 1-866-506-1949 or business@simonandschuster.com.

The Simon & Schuster Speakers Bureau can bring authors to your live event. For more information or to book an event contact the Simon & Schuster Speakers Bureau at 1-866-248-3049 or visit our website at www.simonspeakers.com.

Interior design by Erin Alexander
Illustrations by Claudia Wolf; © 123RF
Photographs by Harper Point Photography
Photography chefs: Martine English, Christine Tarango

Manufactured in the United States of America

1 2022

Library of Congress Cataloging-in-Publication Data has been applied for.

ISBN 978-1-5072-1991-1
ISBN 978-1-5072-1992-8 (ebook)

Dedication

To my amazing husband, Dave,
my favorite sous chef, taster, and dishwasher.

Contents

Chapter 3

Pies and Tarts | 49

Chapter 4

Breakfast Sweets | 65

Chapter 5

Cookies and Bars | 79

Chapter 6

Trifles, Puddings, and Parfaits | 99

Chapter 7

Ice Creams, Frappés, and Drinks | 111

Chapter 8

Confections and Treats | 125

Acknowledgments

I couldn't have written this without a little help from a lot of people. First, many thanks to my taste-testers, Dave Whitney, Keith Downey, the Jennings family, and Michael Biggs; my cheerleaders/accountability coaches, Jennifer Keishin Armstrong, Michelle Terwilleger, and Alexa Chigounis; and my aebleskiver pan lenders, Shelley and David Mamann. Many thanks to my agent, Adam Chromy, and to Eileen Mullan, Sarah Doughty, and all the editors, illustrators, and subcontractors at Adams Media. And, last but not least, many thanks to the Strawberry Shortcake Fandom, who is the Berry Best, now and forever.

Introduction

Welcome to Strawberryland!

In this magical place, berries grow as big as beach balls, animals talk, the sun grants wishes, a snail delivers your mail, and butterflies double as airplanes. Best of all, everyone is obsessed with food, particularly sweet foods like fruits and berries, and cakes, cookies, and pies! Most notable is heroine Strawberry Shortcake, Strawberryland's most popular resident. Strawberry is an avid baker and dedicated strawberry farmer whose crop supplies most of the area. When she's not working hard, she loves spending time with her friends, including best friend, Blueberry Muffin, and sharing a sweet treat with them.

In *The Unofficial Strawberry Shortcake Cookbook*, you're invited to spend as much time as you like with Strawberry and her friends, and make seventy-five delicious goodies crafted in their honor! You'll find all types of sweets, such as:

- Cakes, including (of course) Strawberry Shortcake and Lime's Dancing Chiffon Cake
- Pastries and fancy desserts, such as Blushing Peach Turnovers and Pearis's Best Mini Éclairs
- Pies and tarts, like Huckleberry's Pie and Marmalade's Fluttering Pastry Cups
- Breakfast sweets, such as Pupcake's Pancake Puffs and Hopsalot's Carrot Cake Muffins
- Cookies and bars, like Bourbon Mint Tulip Sandwich Cookies and Maple Stirrup Blondies
- Trifles, puddings, and parfaits, including Custard's Strawberry Panna Cotta and Strawberry Charlotte

- Ice creams, frappés, and drinks, like Ada's Lemon Drop Granita and Berry Scary Blueberry Milkshakes
- And confections and treats, including Marza Panda's Marzipan Bites and Crispy Marshmallow Lucky Bugs

You don't have to be a skilled cook like Crepe Suzette to make these goodies! Although if you *do* want to practice your culinary talents—and show the envious Purple Pieman how it's done—there are a number of fancy recipes to enjoy, like Berry Bake Shoppe Strawberry Napoleons and Stop-and-Go Grape Clafoutis. And there are lots of recipes to make and enjoy as a family, like Butterfly Cupcakes and Coco Nutwork's Coconut Chocolate Oatmeal Orbs.

Most of all, enjoy your trip to Strawberryland! Because even if you can't stay for as long as you'd like, it will stay in your heart forever.

Chapter 1

Cakes

Most people would consider cake a treat for a special occasion, but Strawberry Shortcake and her friends prove that spending time with someone you love is *always* a special occasion. And who are we to argue with someone who has the word "cake" in her name?

Ironically, shortcakes, being less sweet, are more closely related to scones or biscuits than to cakes. But Strawberry is an independent sort and a born leader, so we would not deny her the first entry in this chapter. And there are plenty of other recipes that satisfy the strictest cake definition, from Orange Blossom Layer Cake, to Apricot's Chocolate Jam Cake, to Raspberry Tart's Raspberry Chocolate Torte. And then, there's Cheesecake Mouse's Blueberry Ginger Temptation, inspired by Blueberry Muffin's pet. Looking for something lighter? Try the Perfectly Polite Angel Food Cake.

Strawberry Shortcake

Strawberry's signature dessert has everything it needs to make it a perennial favorite: fresh strawberries, sweet and airy clouds of whipped cream, and a not-too-sweet pastry that lets the other flavors shine through. It also reflects this berry sweet girl's personality: Strawberry is generous and kind and quick to make friends! Add some flowers for an extra sweet presentation.

Serves 6

For Shortcake

1½ cups plus 1½ tablespoons
    all-purpose flour, divided
⅔ cup granulated sugar
4 tablespoons unsalted butter
1 large egg, room temperature
1 teaspoon vanilla extract
¼ teaspoon salt
2 teaspoons baking powder
½ cup whole milk

For Berries

1½ cups sliced fresh strawberries
1½ tablespoons lemon juice (or
    1½ tablespoons Marsala)
1½ tablespoons granulated sugar

For Topping

1½ cups heavy cream
1½ tablespoons cream cheese
3 tablespoons confectioners' sugar
6 large whole fresh strawberries

1. To make Shortcake: Preheat oven to 350°F. Grease three round 6" cake pans with butter and dust each pan with ½ tablespoon flour.

2. In a large bowl, cream sugar and butter. Stir in egg and vanilla. In a separate medium bowl, combine salt, remaining 1½ cups flour, and baking powder. Stir dry ingredients into wet ingredients gradually, alternating with milk.

3. Spread batter into prepared pans. Bake 15–20 minutes until golden.

4. Cool Shortcake 10 minutes in pans, then remove from pans onto a wire rack to cool 1 hour.

5. To make Berries: Combine strawberry slices, lemon juice (or Marsala), and sugar in a medium bowl.

6. To make Topping: Whip cream and cream cheese in a large chilled bowl with chilled beaters until soft peaks form; add sugar, continuing to whip until peaks stiffen.

7. To assemble: Trim any domes off each shortcake layer to get an even surface. Spread ⅓ whipped cream on 1 cake layer. Top with half of Berries. Top with second cake layer, another ⅓ whipped cream, and remaining Berries. Top with third cake layer, and spread remaining whipped cream on top. Garnish with whole strawberries. Chill 20 minutes then cut into wedges and serve.

Orange Blossom Layer Cake

Orange Blossom first befriends Strawberry Shortcake during Strawberry's trip to Big Apple City (*Strawberry Shortcake in Big Apple City*, 1981). She is a talented artist with a great zest for life. This orange layer cake embodies that zest, with a light vanilla cake, tangy marmalade filling, and orange buttercream frosting.

Serves 8

For Cakes
2 tablespoons all-purpose flour
1 cup (2 sticks) unsalted butter,
    room temperature
2 cups granulated sugar
4 large eggs
1 tablespoon baking powder
¼ teaspoon salt
1¾ cups 2% milk
1 tablespoon vanilla extract
3½ cups cake flour

For Frosting
½ cup (1 stick) unsalted butter,
    room temperature
3¾ cups confectioners' sugar
2 tablespoons pulp-free orange juice
Zest of 1 large orange
3 drops orange food coloring

For Filling
¾ cup orange marmalade

For Fondant Blossoms
1 (4.4-ounce) package white
    vanilla fondant
4 drops orange food coloring

1. To make Cakes: Preheat oven to 325°F. Grease two round 8" cake pans with butter and dust each pan with 1 tablespoon all-purpose flour.

2. Cream together butter and sugar in a large bowl until fluffy. Add eggs one at a time, mixing well to combine, scraping down sides of bowl as needed. Stir in baking powder and salt.

3. Mix milk and vanilla. Alternate adding cake flour and milk to bowl while mixing, finishing with flour. Mix until batter is smooth.

4. Divide batter among prepared pans. Bake 35–50 minutes, until a toothpick inserted in center comes out clean. Cool Cakes in pans 10 minutes before removing from pans and transferring to a wire rack.

5. To make Frosting: Beat butter in a medium bowl until fluffy. Gradually beat in sugar until well combined. Add orange juice and zest. Stir in food coloring.

6. Cover top of 1 Cake with marmalade. Top with second Cake, pressing down gently. Frost top and sides.

7. To make Fondant Blossoms: Pinch off 1 tablespoon fondant and combine with food coloring. Knead until color is evenly distributed. Set aside.

8. Roll out white fondant on a surface dusted with confectioners' sugar to ⅛" thickness. Cut out forty ½" petals and eight ¼" circles. Arrange five petals in a star shape near edge of top of Cake (or around sides if preferred), then press a circle in middle of petals. Roll orange fondant into tiny balls (about the size of a chia seed), and press four balls onto each white blossom circle. Repeat with some remaining fondant to create a larger flower. Arrange large flower on center of cake and remaining flowers along the top edge.

Raspberry Tart's Raspberry Chocolate Torte

Raspberry Tart is one of Strawberry's close friends. Over the years, she has gone from being called Raspberry Tart to Raspberry Torte and then back again. This Raspberry Chocolate Torte celebrates those little idiosyncrasies that keep life in *and* out of Strawberryland interesting, with its light chocolate cake, rich ganache topping, and berry cream filling.

Serves 8

For Cake
1¾ cups plus 2 tablespoons
    all-purpose flour, divided
2 cups granulated sugar
¾ cup cocoa powder
1½ teaspoons baking powder
1½ teaspoons baking soda
1 teaspoon salt
1 teaspoon ground cinnamon
2 large eggs
1 cup 2% milk
½ cup vegetable oil
2 teaspoons vanilla extract
¼ cup freshly brewed espresso
    or very strong coffee
¾ cup boiling water

For Filling
½ cup heavy whipping cream
1 tablespoon confectioners' sugar
2 tablespoons raspberry preserves

For Topping
12 ounces bittersweet chocolate,
    finely chopped
1½ cups heavy cream
2 teaspoons raspberry liqueur
1 cup fresh raspberries

1. To make Cake: Preheat oven to 350°F. Grease two 8" cake pans with butter and dust each pan with 1 tablespoon flour.

2. Whisk together sugar, remaining 1¾ cups flour, cocoa, baking powder, baking soda, salt, and cinnamon in a large bowl. Stir in eggs, milk, vegetable oil, and vanilla. Stir in coffee and boiling water.

3. Divide batter evenly among prepared pans and bake 30–40 minutes until a toothpick inserted in center comes out clean. Cool 10 minutes in pans, then remove from pan onto a wire rack and cool completely, 45–60 minutes, before filling and topping.

4. To make Filling: Whip cream into soft peaks in a chilled medium bowl. Add sugar, and continue whipping until stiff peaks appear. Fold in raspberry preserves.

5. To make Topping: Place chocolate in a medium heatproof bowl. Place cream in a small saucepan and heat over medium heat until little bubbles form on the sides, about 3 minutes. Do not let it boil.

6. Pour hot cream over chocolate and stir until mixture is smooth and glossy. Stir in liqueur. Let cool and thicken 45 minutes before using.

7. Spread Filling on 1 Cake, then top with second Cake. Pour Topping onto Cake and spread evenly over top and sides. Garnish with raspberries. Refrigerate 30 minutes before serving.

Apple's Big Birthday Cake

Apple Dumplin' may be one of Strawberryland's babies, but she's still brave enough to help defeat the Purple Pieman (*The World of Strawberry Shortcake*, 1980). In *Meet Strawberry Shortcake* (2003), she has a big birthday coming up, and older sister Strawberry puts on a party for her. This cake pays tribute to Apple's sweet and spicy personality, with its fruit-filled batter and rich cream cheese frosting. Best of all, it can be served for any occasion—not just a birthday!

Serves 12

For Cake
2 cups plus 2 tablespoons
    all-purpose flour, divided
2 cups granulated sugar
½ cup canola oil
2 large eggs
2 teaspoons vanilla extract
1 teaspoon ground cinnamon
½ teaspoon ground cardamom
½ teaspoon ground ginger
¼ teaspoon ground cloves
¼ teaspoon ground nutmeg
¼ teaspoon ground allspice
2 teaspoons baking powder
1 teaspoon salt
½ cup sour cream
1½ pounds yellow-red apples,
    peeled, cored, and finely chopped
1½ cups chopped walnuts

For Frosting
¾ cup (1½ sticks) unsalted butter
12 ounces cream cheese
5 cups confectioners' sugar
2 tablespoons whole milk
1½ teaspoons vanilla extract
1½ teaspoons ground cinnamon

1. To make Cake: Preheat oven to 350°F. Grease two 8" cake pans with butter and dust each pan with 1 tablespoon flour.

2. Mix sugar, oil, eggs, and vanilla in a large bowl. Stir in spices, baking powder, and salt. Stir in remaining 2 cups flour and sour cream. Stir in apples and walnuts.

3. Divide batter among prepared pans and bake 35–50 minutes until a toothpick inserted in center comes out clean. Cool in pans 10 minutes, then unmold onto a cooling rack and cool completely, 45–60 minutes. Freeze 30 minutes.

4. To make Frosting: Mix butter and cream cheese in a medium bowl. Gradually add sugar, stirring until Frosting comes together. If Frosting is too thick, add milk to thin it. Stir in vanilla and cinnamon.

5. Cut each Cake into two layers. Frost top of three layers. Top with last layer. Frost top and sides of Cake. Refrigerate 1 hour before serving.

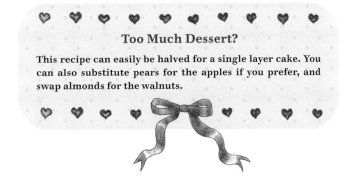

Too Much Dessert?

This recipe can easily be halved for a single layer cake. You can also substitute pears for the apples if you prefer, and swap almonds for the walnuts.

Cheesecake Mouse's Blueberry Ginger Temptation

Blueberry Muffin's pet, Cheesecake, inspires this dessert; what mouse doesn't love cheese? Both mice and humans in your family will like this recipe, which adds some flair to the usual cheesecake fare. It features a ginger cookie crust, tangy topping, and a little octane in the creamy filling—which also includes mascarpone cheese and crème fraîche.

Serves 12

For Crust
2 cups ground ginger cookies
2 tablespoons granulated sugar
6 tablespoons unsalted butter,
    melted

For Filling
2 cups fresh blueberries
1 cup plus 2 tablespoons granulated
    sugar, divided
1 tablespoon plus 1 teaspoon
    Cointreau, divided
16 ounces cream cheese, room
    temperature
16 ounces mascarpone cheese, room
    temperature
2 large eggs
1 teaspoon vanilla extract
Zest of 1 large orange
¼ cup crème fraîche
2 tablespoons all-purpose flour
¼ teaspoon salt

For Blueberry Coulis
3 cups fresh blueberries, divided
2 tablespoons granulated sugar
2 teaspoons lemon juice

1. To make Crust: Preheat oven to 350°F. Grease a 9" springform pan with butter.

2. Combine ginger cookie crumbs and sugar in a medium bowl. Stir in melted butter. Press mixture into prepared pan, covering bottom and pressing up sides.

3. Bake Crust 20 minutes until puffed and golden. Remove from oven and reduce oven to 325°F.

4. To make Filling: Purée blueberries in a food processor. Pour purée into a small saucepan and add 2 tablespoons sugar and 1 tablespoon Cointreau. Stir to dissolve sugar, then bring mixture to a boil over high heat. Reduce heat to medium-low and cook until mixture thickens, about 10 minutes. Cool to room temperature, 30–45 minutes.

5. Beat cream cheese, mascarpone, and remaining 1 cup sugar in a large bowl until smooth. Stir in eggs, vanilla, remaining 1 teaspoon Cointreau, orange zest, and crème fraîche. Stir in flour, salt, and cooled blueberry purée.

6. Pour Filling into Crust and smooth top. Wrap pan snugly in aluminum foil and place in a large roasting pan. Pour enough boiling water into roasting pan to come 1" up springform pan. Bake cheesecake 90 minutes or until Filling has set.

7. Remove springform pan from water bath. Peel off aluminum foil, and cool on a wire rack 1 hour. Refrigerate at least 6 hours, up to overnight.

8. To make Blueberry Coulis: Purée 2 cups blueberries in a food processor. Pour into a small saucepan along with sugar and lemon juice. Stir until sugar is dissolved, then bring to a boil over high heat. Reduce heat to medium-low and cook, stirring occasionally, until thickened. Cool completely, 30–45 minutes.

9. Remove cheesecake from pan and top with Blueberry Coulis and remaining 1 cup blueberries.

Apricot's Chocolate Jam Cake

An apricot jam filling and a tangy apricot buttercream frosting make this chocolate layer cake a special treat worthy of Strawberry's friend, the precocious baby Apricot (who has a more impressive vocabulary than many adults). Apricot is introduced in *Strawberry Shortcake in Big Apple City* (1981), and she moves to Strawberryland after, along with several other friends. The dried apricots and mint leaves in this recipe add a decorative touch reminiscent of the signature hat that usually covers Apricot's curly white hair.

Serves 8

For Cake

1¼ cups plus 2 tablespoons
    all-purpose flour, divided
2 cups granulated sugar
¾ cup cocoa powder
1½ teaspoons baking powder
1½ teaspoons baking soda
1 teaspoon salt
2 large eggs
1 cup 2% milk
½ cup vegetable oil
2 teaspoons vanilla extract
¼ cup freshly brewed espresso
    or very strong coffee
¾ cup boiling water

For Frosting

½ cup (1 stick) unsalted butter,
    softened
3¾ cups confectioners' sugar
½ cup apricot jam
1 teaspoon Cointreau
2 teaspoons vanilla extract
7 dried apricots
7 small mint leaves

For Filling

¾ cup apricot jam

1. To make Cake: Preheat oven to 350°F. Grease two 8" cake pans with butter and dust each pan with 1 tablespoon flour.

2. Whisk together sugar, remaining 1¼ cups flour, cocoa, baking powder, baking soda, and salt in a large bowl. Stir in eggs, milk, oil, and vanilla. Stir in coffee and boiling water.

3. Divide batter evenly among prepared pans and bake 30–40 minutes, until a toothpick inserted in center comes out clean. Cool Cakes 10 minutes before removing from pans onto a wire rack. Cool completely, 45–60 minutes.

4. To make Frosting: Beat butter and sugar in a medium bowl until smooth. Stir in apricot jam, Cointreau, and vanilla. If Frosting is too runny, add more sugar.

5. Spread apricot jam filling evenly on top of one Cake layer and top with second Cake layer. Frost top and sides of Cake. Decorate edges of Cake top (or around Cake bottom, if preferred) with dried apricots, tucking a small mint leaf under top edge of each apricot.

Let Them Eat Cupcakes!

This recipe also works well as cupcakes; it yields twenty-four, and bakes at the same temperature for 15–20 minutes, until a toothpick inserted in center comes out clean.

Lime's Dancing Chiffon Cake

Lime Chiffon is Strawberryland's most dedicated ballerina, and like dancers everywhere, she is light, but also flexible and strong. This cake inspired by her name fits those criteria. Chiffon cakes, which include egg yolks, are not quite as fragile as their close cousins, angel food cakes, even though both are baked in the same kind of footed tube pan. Chiffon cakes also bear up well under frostings and fillings, and this one is complemented wonderfully by a lime curd filling. Top it with a dollop of whipped cream!

Serves 10

For Cake
7 large eggs, room temperature
¼ cup water
½ cup vegetable oil
½ cup lime juice
1 teaspoon vanilla extract
1½ cups granulated sugar
3 teaspoons baking powder
½ teaspoon salt
1¾ cups all-purpose flour
½ teaspoon cream of tartar

For Assembly
¾ cup lime curd
2 tablespoons confectioners' sugar

1. To make Cake: Preheat oven to 325°F.

2. Separate eggs, placing whites in bowl of an electric mixer and yolks in a large mixing bowl.

3. Add water, oil, lime juice, vanilla, and sugar to egg yolks and whisk to combine. Stir in baking powder and salt. Stir in flour.

4. Add cream of tartar to egg whites and beat until stiff peaks form.

5. Fold egg whites into batter gradually, making sure not to deflate the mixture. (The batter will double in size.)

6. Pour batter into an ungreased fluted two-piece angel food cake pan, smooth top, and bake 45–60 minutes, until top is golden and springs back when touched. (Touch lightly, or you may dent the Cake!)

7. Invert cake pan and let cool 2 hours. Run knife along the sides and flute. Remove from pan and use knife to free Cake from bottom part of the pan. Invert Cake on a platter.

8. To assemble: Cut Cake into two horizontal layers using a serrated knife. Spread lime curd on bottom layer and top with second layer. Dust with sugar and serve.

Caterpillar Cakes

Several large caterpillars play supporting roles in Strawberryland, including the Berry Busy Bug and Mr. Longface. Cake pops (or in this case cake balls, as there are no lollipop sticks) are a fun and tasty way to depict these characters. This hands-on recipe is sure to be a hit—especially with younger bakers, who will enjoy making and decorating these quirky cakes.

Serves 12

For Cakes

1 (13" × 19") red velvet cake
2 cups cream cheese frosting
48 ounces white chocolate, chopped
4 drops teal food coloring
4 drops green food coloring

For Decorating

1 ounce white fondant
2 ounces brown fondant
2 (4.4-ounce) packages blue fondant

1. To make Cakes: Crumble up red velvet cake in a big mixing bowl until cake becomes fine crumbs. Add 2 heaping tablespoons of frosting and stir. Keep adding frosting until a handful of crumbs holds its shape without falling apart.

2. Line a large baking sheet with wax paper. With an ice cream scoop, scoop out the crumb mixture and roll each into a 1½" ball. You should have at least thirty-six balls. Place on baking sheet and freeze 3 hours.

3. Place white chocolate in a medium microwave-safe bowl. Either melt over a water bath or in microwave in 10-second intervals, stirring between cook times, until smooth. Divide into two bowls. Stir teal food coloring into one bowl and green food coloring into the other.

4. Line two baking sheets with wax paper. Remove cake balls from freezer. Dip half of cake balls in teal chocolate and other half of cake balls in green chocolate. Arrange balls snugly against each other on baking sheets in alternating colors, using six cake balls per caterpillar.

5. To Decorate: Make eyes using white fondant for the irises and brown fondant for the pupils. Use brown fondant for the mouths. If necessary, use a bit of leftover frosting to attach eyes and mouths to the caterpillar heads.

6. To make hats, roll out one package blue fondant to ¼" thick. Cut out six ¾"-wide circles. Use some of remaining fondant to shape six ½"-wide by 1"-tall cylinders. Center a cylinder on top of each circle to make a hat, then place hats on caterpillar heads, using frosting to attach if necessary. Use remaining blue fondant to make small dots and place along caterpillar bodies. Allow Cakes to set 1 hour at room temperature before serving.

Butterfly Cupcakes

Butterflies are a big part of Strawberryland's ecosystem, and come in various magical sizes, from Flitter-Bit, who is giant enough to serve as a small airplane for Strawberry and her friends, to Orange Blossom's bird-sized butterfly, Marmalade. Like the lovely insects, these Butterfly Cupcakes have wings, which are nestled in a bed of citrus curd (or jam) and buttercream and dusted with rainbow sprinkles.

Makes 24 cupcakes

24 yellow cupcakes
3¼ cups vanilla buttercream,
    divided
3 drops red food coloring
1 cup lemon curd (or jam of choice)
2 tablespoons rainbow sprinkles

1. Carefully cut out the center of each cupcake, making sure to angle the knife at 45 degrees. Remove center, and cut in half to resemble butterfly wings.

2. In a medium bowl, mix 3 cups buttercream and food coloring. Fill each cupcake indentation with 2 tablespoons red buttercream, then make a small dent in buttercream and spoon curd into center of buttercream, in the shape of a butterfly's body.

3. Carefully spread remaining ¼ cup buttercream on smooth sides of cupcake "wings." Garnish with sprinkles. Arrange wings on top of cupcakes, on either side of curd "bodies."

Oh, the Possibilities!

Any flavor cupcake, frosting, or filling can be used here. For chocolate, try the cake recipe from Apricot's Chocolate Jam Cake in this chapter. Divide the batter among twenty-four cupcake or muffin tins, and bake 15–20 minutes until a toothpick inserted in the center comes out clean. You can also use sweetened whipped cream instead of frosting.

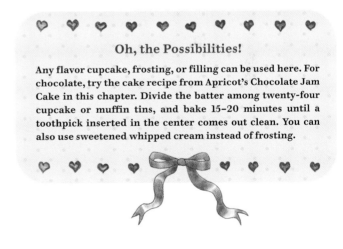

Bird's Nest Cupcakes

Birds are popular pets in Strawberryland, from Plum Puddin's Elderberry Owl to Lime Chiffon's Parfait Parrot. These cute little cupcakes become bird's nests with some frosting, shredded dyed coconut, and your choice of candy eggs. Make sure to eat them before a bird tries to move in!

Makes 24 cupcakes

2 cups shredded coconut
3 drops green food coloring
24 chocolate cupcakes
3 cups vanilla buttercream
72 jelly beans or chocolate eggs

1. Place shredded coconut in a shallow dish. Add a few drops of food coloring and stir with a fork until coconut is evenly dyed.

2. Frost each cupcake with 2 tablespoons buttercream, then smooth the top. Dip top in the coconut.

3. Nestle 3 jelly beans or chocolate eggs in the middle of each cupcake.

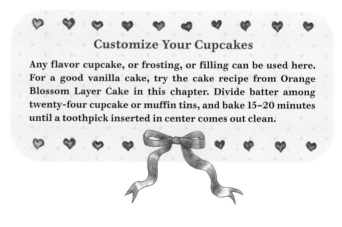

Customize Your Cupcakes

Any flavor cupcake, or frosting, or filling can be used here. For a good vanilla cake, try the cake recipe from Orange Blossom Layer Cake in this chapter. Divide batter among twenty-four cupcake or muffin tins, and bake 15–20 minutes until a toothpick inserted in center comes out clean.

Perfectly Polite Angel Food Cake

Angel Cake moves to Strawberryland shortly before the big annual pet talent show (*Strawberry Shortcake: Pets on Parade*, 1982). Angel often worries about living up to her name, which is why she is exceedingly polite, and she frets about calories, even as she eats candy constantly (she claims those calories don't count). Angel food cake is perfectly representative of her, being fat-free but still wonderfully sweet. This recipe is delicious plain, but can also be served with blueberry coulis and vanilla sauce.

Serves 8

12 large egg whites,
    room temperature
1 teaspoon cream of tartar
1¼ cups granulated sugar
1 teaspoon vanilla extract
1 teaspoon lemon juice
¼ teaspoon salt
1 cup cake flour

1. Preheat oven to 350°F.

2. Beat egg whites in a large bowl until they start to bubble and thicken. Add cream of tartar, still beating, until soft peaks form. Add sugar gradually while beating until stiff peaks form. Stir in vanilla, lemon juice, and salt.

3. Sift flour and fold into egg whites ¼ cup at a time.

4. Transfer batter to an ungreased fluted angel food cake pan. Smooth top. Using a spatula or knife, stab batter a few times to get rid of air bubbles.

5. Bake 35–40 minutes until top is golden. Invert pan and cool 1 hour.

6. To remove cake from pan, run a knife around the fluted tube and sides, then cut around bottom to release fully. Invert on a serving platter. Serve.

Too Many Yolks?

Consider using any extra egg yolks to make pastry cream (see Raspberry's Not-So-Tart Tarts recipe in Chapter 3) for the Berry Princess's Tutti-Frutti Trifle (see recipe in Chapter 6).

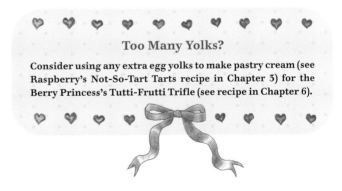

Mr. Sun's Saffron Cake

In Strawberryland, the sun is not just a source of heat and light, but is known as Mr. Sun. He is the narrator, sometime giver of wishes, and loyal friend to the kids. This Saffron Cake is as bright as its namesake, not just because of its golden batter, but also because of its almond-flavored icing with a pretty sunburst design. Try out different decorations for the face, like using yellow icing to pipe the mouth, eyebrows, and nose!

Serves 8

For Cake
2 tablespoons unseasoned fine
    bread crumbs
2 large eggs
1¼ cups granulated sugar
0.025 ounces saffron threads,
    ground to powder
2 teaspoons baking powder
⅔ cup whole milk
1¾ cups all-purpose flour
14 tablespoons salted butter, melted

For Topping
2 cups confectioners' sugar, sifted
9 teaspoons water
1 teaspoon almond extract
3 drops yellow food coloring
1 ounce white fondant
2 ounces brown fondant

1. To make Cake: Preheat oven to 350°F. Grease the inside of a 9" springform pan with butter, then coat with bread crumbs.

2. In a medium bowl, beat eggs and sugar together until very pale and thick. Add saffron, baking powder, and milk. Stir gently. Add flour and melted butter and stir until batter is just combined.

3. Scrape batter into prepared springform pan. Bake on a low rack for 35–45 minutes or until Cake is golden on top and is pulling away a bit from the sides. Toothpick inserted in center of Cake should come out clean. Allow Cake to cool 10 minutes before removing from the pan onto a large plate. Ice Cake only after it has cooled completely, 45–60 minutes.

4. To make Topping: Mix sugar, water, and extract into a smooth, not runny paste.

5. Pour half the icing on top of Cake. Spread to cover, trying not to let icing drip over the sides.

6. Add food coloring to remaining icing. Pour yellow icing onto the center, trying to keep it a rough circle 5" wide. Using the tip of a sharp knife, draw yellow icing toward edges, making sun rays. Use more icing to outline sun and create a mouth, nose, and eyebrows. Let icing set 1 hour.

7. Shape white fondant into two eyes and shape brown fondant into irises, eyebrows, a nose, and a mouth. Arrange on top of icing.

Berrykin Princess Cakes

The Berrykins are the scent purveyors of Strawberryland and obey the Berry Princess (*Strawberry Shortcake Meets the Berrykins*, 1985). She is a fair and steadfast ruler, and these little pink marzipan-covered cakes, filled with jam and cream, are a perfect tribute to her Highness. This recipe is also inspired by Sweden's most famous cake, the princess cake, said to be favored by the country's princesses in the mid-twentieth century.

Serves 12

4 drops red food coloring
28 ounces marzipan
1 (9" × 13") yellow sheet cake
½ cup raspberry preserves
2½ cups heavy whipping cream
2½ tablespoons cream cheese
½ cup plus ½ tablespoon
    confectioners' sugar, divided
⅓ cup fresh strawberries,
    blueberries, or raspberries

1. Freeze a medium electric mixer bowl and beaters 30 minutes.

2. On a flat surface, knead food coloring into marzipan by hand until evenly distributed. Cover marzipan with wax paper so it doesn't dry out.

3. Cut twelve 3" rounds out of sheet cake. With a serrated knife, slice each round into two horizontal layers.

4. Spread 1 teaspoon raspberry preserves on half the rounds and top with second layer of cake.

5. Beat cream and cream cheese until soft peaks form. Add ½ cup sugar and beat until stiff peaks form.

6. Dust work surface with remaining ½ tablespoon sugar. Take piece of marzipan, roll out to a rough 8" circle, making sure it doesn't tear or stick. If it sticks, add more sugar.

7. Place rolled-out marzipan on a piece of wax paper. Transfer one of the filled cake rounds to sugared work surface. Place heaping tablespoon of the whipped cream on top of cake. Handling marzipan sheet carefully, drape over cake and press snugly against the sides. Cut away excess marzipan and use for the next cake. Place finished cakes on a large platter.

8. To Decorate: Swirl a teaspoon of leftover whipped cream on top of each cake. Top cream with a half strawberry or a few raspberries or blueberries.

The Right Cake Stuff

The texture of your cake makes a big difference in this recipe. You want a light cake that cuts cleanly and doesn't crumble. Try the cake recipe from Orange Blossom Layer Cake (see earlier in this chapter), baking it in a 9" × 13" pan for 40 minutes at 325°F or until toothpick inserted in center comes out clean.

Chapter 2

Pastry and Fancy Desserts

Home cooks are all too often intimidated by soufflés, flambés, or anything that involves a pastry dough. But Strawberry Shortcake and her chef friend, Crepe Suzette (and of course Crepe's poodle, Éclair), are here to reassure you there's no need to be!

In this chapter, you'll find easy-to-follow recipes for fancy desserts, and tips for simplifying treats that are traditionally a bit more complex. For example, the Berry Bake Shoppe Strawberry Napoleons recipe uses premade puff pastry, as does Little Sister's Spicy Apple Dumplings recipe. And while cream puff pastry might sound tricky, it comes together very quickly, and the resulting Pearis's Best Mini Éclairs (with coffee and chocolate variations!) are as elegant as they are delicious. Whip up one of these desserts the next time you want to impress your boss or friends, have a party, or even one to attend, or just want to end dinner with a flourish!

Berry Bake Shoppe Strawberry Napoleons

Like all the trendiest farm-to-table places, Strawberry's Berry Bake Shoppe has a berry patch just a few steps from the kitchen. Strawberry Napoleons are an impressive and easy way to showcase Strawberry Shortcake's harvest. Unlike regular napoleons (also known as mille-feuilles, or thousand-sheet/layer/leaf cakes), which feature puff pastry layered with pastry cream and topped with a chocolate swirled icing, this recipe lightens the pastry cream with whipped cream, adds berries, and omits the icing in favor of a light dusting of confectioners' sugar.

Serves 12

2 (9¾" × 10½") sheets frozen
   puff pastry, thawed
1 cup vanilla pudding (or pastry cream;
   see Raspberry's Not-So-Tart Tarts
   recipe in Chapter 3)
½ cup whipping cream
3 tablespoons confectioners' sugar,
   divided
1 cup thinly sliced fresh
   strawberries

Think Outside the Strawberry

This recipe is just as tasty with blueberries, raspberries, or blackberries, or a combination of all three!

1. Preheat oven to 400°F.

2. Cut each pastry sheet into three equal rectangles. Place on two parchment paper–lined baking sheets. With a fork, prick pastry rectangles all over (this will help them rise evenly). Refrigerate 30 minutes.

3. Bake 20–25 minutes until puffed and golden. Cool completely, about 30 minutes.

4. Using chilled beaters, whip cream in a large, chilled bowl until soft peaks form. Add 1 tablespoon sugar, and continue beating until stiff peaks appear. Fold in pudding gradually, making sure whipped cream doesn't lose volume.

5. Spread one puff pastry rectangle with a thin layer of cream. Top with a thin layer of strawberries, then add another, thicker layer of cream. Top with second rectangle and press down gently. Top second rectangle with a thin layer of cream, then strawberries, then thicker layer of cream. Top with third pastry layer, press down gently, and set aside. Repeat procedure with remaining pastry and ingredients to create 2 large Napoleons total.

6. Refrigerate Napoleons 30 minutes before serving, then dust with remaining 2 tablespoons sugar. Use a serrated knife to cut each Napoleon into six pieces.

Pearis's Best Mini Éclairs

Make these labor-intensive, but delicious treats in honor of your favorite pup: Crepe Suzette's poodle, Éclair. The word *éclair* means "flash of lightning" in French and reflects how quickly these treats usually last once they're ready. Made of cream puff pastry, filled with custard, and topped with a light icing, these mini éclairs are closest to the kinds you'd find in a Parisian (ahem, Pearisian) patisserie.

Makes 12 éclairs

For Cream Puff Pastry
⅔ cup all-purpose flour
3 tablespoons unsalted butter
½ cup water
2 teaspoons granulated sugar
¼ teaspoon salt
2 large eggs, lightly beaten

For Pastry Cream
¾ cup whole milk
2 large egg yolks
3 tablespoons granulated sugar
1 tablespoon cornstarch
1 teaspoon vanilla extract

For Icing
1 cup confectioners' sugar, sifted
4½ teaspoons water
½ teaspoon vanilla extract

♥ ♥ ♥ ♥ ♥ ♥ ♥
Eclairs with More *Saveur*

To make Coffee Éclairs: Add 2 teaspoons instant coffee to pastry cream (or more to taste) and stir to combine. Substitute strongly brewed coffee for water in icing. To make Chocolate Éclairs: Use your favorite chocolate pudding for filling. Substitute 1 tablespoon confectioners' sugar with cocoa in icing.

♥ ♥ ♥ ♥ ♥ ♥ ♥

---

1. To make Cream Puff Pastry: Preheat oven to 350°F. Line a baking sheet with parchment paper.

2. Sift flour onto wax paper.

3. Combine butter, water, sugar, and salt in a medium saucepan over high heat. Bring to a boil and add all the flour at once. Take pan off the heat. Stir with wooden spoon until a rough dough forms. Return to heat and stir while working dough into a ball.

4. Place dough in a bowl and, using a wooden spoon, mix in eggs gradually until dough is smooth and glossy. Transfer dough to piping bag with a wide tip and pipe twelve (3") éclairs onto baking sheet.

5. Bake 30–35 minutes or until éclairs are puffed, golden, and dough looks a bit dry.

6. To make Pastry Cream: Whisk together milk, egg yolks, sugar, and cornstarch in a small heavy-bottomed pan. Keep whisking constantly over medium-low heat until it boils and thickens, about 10 minutes. Cool 45–60 minutes before adding vanilla.

7. To make Icing: Mix sugar, water, and vanilla into a smooth, not too runny paste.

8. To assemble: Cut each Pastry in half horizontally using serrated knife. Place a tablespoon of Pastry Cream in bottom half and top with second half of Pastry. Spread Icing on top. Allow Icing to set 30 minutes before serving.

Little Sister's Spicy Apple Dumplings

Apple Dumplin's signature dessert, Apple Dumplings, is as satisfying and classic as Strawberry's shortcake. The trick to making sure the apples cook thoroughly before their pastry shell burns is to core them, slice them, and restack them. And don't skimp on the sugar and spice! After all, being the younger sibling of the best baker in Strawberryland means having some awfully big baking tins to fill!

Makes 6 dumplings

2 (9¾" × 10½") sheets frozen
    puff pastry
1 cup plus 4 tablespoons dark
    brown sugar, divided
½ teaspoon ground ginger
½ teaspoon ground cardamom
¼ teaspoon ground nutmeg
¼ teaspoon ground cloves
3 large sweet yellow or red apples
    (such as Fuji)
1 cup water
2 tablespoons salted butter
½ teaspoon ground cinnamon

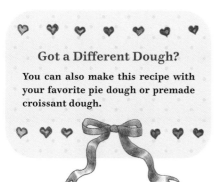

Got a Different Dough?

You can also make this recipe with your favorite pie dough or premade croissant dough.

1. Thaw puff pastry sheets 30–45 minutes, then cut each sheet into four equal squares. Roll out six squares to about twice their size, ⅛" thick.

2. Preheat oven to 350°F.

3. Combine 4 tablespoons sugar, ginger, cardamom, nutmeg, and cloves in a small bowl and set aside.

4. Peel, core, and slice apples thinly and keep each apple's slices in separate piles. Stack half the slices from each apple on top of one of the bigger pastry squares. Spoon sugar and spice mixture into the middle. Wrap pastry snugly around each apple stack and place each dumpling in an 8" × 11" glass baking dish.

5. Cut out twelve leaf shapes and six stem shapes from remaining dough and arrange one stem and two leaves on top of each dumpling.

6. Place remaining 1 cup sugar, water, butter, and cinnamon in a small saucepan. Heat over medium heat until butter is melted and mixture simmers at the edges. Pour sugar mixture over dumplings (liquid should come about halfway up the dumplings).

7. Bake 45 minutes or until dough is golden and puffy. Serve warm with sweetened whipped cream, vanilla ice cream, or vanilla sauce (see the Record-Breaking Strawberry Soufflés recipe in this chapter).

Blushing Peach Turnovers

Southern belle Peach Blush is Strawberry's friend from The Land of the Magnolias. She and Strawberry meet when she travels to Strawberryland with her friend Plum Puddin' (*Strawberry Shortcake and the Baby Without a Name*, 1984). These turnovers are as refined as she is, made with puff pastry, lightly sweetened peaches, chopped almonds, and a hint of rosewater. For that extra touch of Peach Blush drama, they are sprinkled with pink sugar.

Makes 8 turnovers

4 large peach halves,
    finely chopped
2 tablespoons dark brown sugar
1 tablespoon all-purpose flour
Juice of ½ large lemon
½ teaspoon almond extract
½ teaspoon rosewater extract
2 tablespoons chopped
    toasted almonds
2 tablespoons dried cranberries
2 (9¾" × 10½") sheets frozen
    puff pastry, thawed
1 large egg
1 teaspoon 2% milk
3 tablespoons granulated sugar
2 drops red food coloring

1. Line a baking sheet with parchment paper.

2. Mix peaches with brown sugar, flour, lemon juice, both extracts, almonds, and cranberries in a large bowl.

3. Place each puff pastry sheet on a floured surface. Cut each sheet into four squares and roll out to double the size, about ⅛" thick.

4. Beat together egg and milk in a small bowl. Place peach filling in center of each pastry square. With a pastry brush, paint borders of each square with ¼ egg mixture (set rest aside), then fold one point onto another, forming a triangle. Seal pastry triangle edges with a fork, making sure no filling leaks out.

5. Transfer turnovers to prepared baking sheet. Make sure to space them well apart. Refrigerate 30 minutes.

6. Preheat oven to 400°F.

7. Mix granulated sugar and food coloring in a medium bowl. Paint tops of chilled turnovers with remaining egg mixture, then sprinkle with colored sugar.

8. Bake 15–20 minutes, until turnovers are well puffed and golden. Serve warm or at room temperature.

Blackberry Lemon Failed Soufflé Cake

Soufflé the Skunk becomes Angel Cake's companion after he wins Strawberryland's pet talent show (*Strawberry Shortcake: Pets on Parade*, 1982). Before that, he feels dejected, because few people like skunks. This blackberry lemon cake recipe could be referred to as a "failed soufflé," but is really an example of how something can be wonderful in its own right.

Serves 6

¾ cup plus 1 tablespoon
    granulated sugar, divided
2½ cups fresh blackberries,
    divided
2 tablespoons lemon juice
Zest of 1 large lemon
1 cup buttermilk
½ cup sour cream
3 large eggs
4 tablespoons unsalted butter,
    room temperature
⅓ cup all-purpose flour
¼ teaspoon salt
2 tablespoons confectioners' sugar

1. Grease a shallow 10" baking dish with butter and sprinkle with 1 tablespoon granulated sugar. Preheat oven to 325°F.

2. Purée 1½ cups blackberries in a food processor, then push through a sieve, making sure no seeds get through. Measure out 6 tablespoons of purée and place in a large bowl. (Reserve any leftover purée for serving.) Add lemon juice, lemon zest, buttermilk, and sour cream to purée and mix.

3. Separate eggs, placing yolks in a small bowl and whites in a large bowl.

4. Beat together butter and remaining ¾ cup granulated sugar in a large bowl. Add egg yolks one at a time, beating well after each addition and scraping down sides of bowl. Alternate adding blackberry mixture and flour, stirring well after each addition.

5. Add salt to egg whites and whip until stiff peaks form. Gradually fold whipped egg whites into blackberry batter until smooth but not overly mixed.

6. Transfer batter to prepared baking dish and bake 40–45 minutes until top is golden. Center may still be a little shaky.

7. Cool 30 minutes in dish before serving. Serve dusted with confectioners' sugar and topped with remaining 1 cup whole blackberries and any leftover blackberry purée.

Times Pear Danishes

Whether you're in Times Pear for shopping or a show, competing in a baking contest against a villanous Purple Pieman (*Strawberry Shortcake in Big Apple City*, 1981), or just relaxing at home on a weekend morning, a Times Pear Danish is a must to start the day. These Danishes are not overly complicated to make, using premade puff pastry dough, almond custard, and a simple fruit glaze, but the results are impressively delicious.

Makes 8 Danishes

For Pastry
2 (9¾" × 10½") sheets frozen
    puff pastry, thawed
1 cup vanilla pudding
1 teaspoon almond extract
8 canned pear halves
1 large egg
1 teaspoon water

For Glaze
3 tablespoons apricot jam
1 tablespoon water

For Topping
1 cup confectioners' sugar, sifted
4 teaspoons water
1 teaspoon almond extract
⅓ cup slivered almonds

Not Danish After All!

Though people often think Danishes originated in Denmark, these pastries are known in that country as *wienerbrø*, or "breads from Vienna." The Austrian capital gets the real credit for inventing Danishes, as well as creating other laminated pastries, including croissants, known in France as *viennoiseries* ("pastries from Vienna").

1. To make Pastry: Cut each pastry sheet into four pieces. Roll each piece into a rectangle about twice the original size or until dough is ⅛" thick. Cut one 1" square out of each corner of each rectangle to form tabs, then fold tabs over, making a frame. Roll out again until each rectangle measures about 3" × 5".

2. Mix pudding and almond extract in a medium bowl. Place 2 tablespoons mixture in the center of each rectangle, and place a pear half on top. With a thin spatula, transfer Pastries to a baking sheet lined with aluminum foil and greased with nonstick cooking spray. Refrigerate 30 minutes.

3. Preheat oven to 400°F.

4. Whisk together egg and water in a small bowl. With a pastry brush, paint borders of each chilled Pastry with egg mixture. Bake 20 minutes until puffy and golden. Allow to cool 20 minutes before glazing.

5. To make Glaze: Place jam and water in a small saucepan. Heat mixture over medium heat, stirring, until jam melts and Glaze is bubbling slightly, about 5 minutes. Remove from heat and paint each pear and surrounding cream with Glaze.

6. To make Topping: Mix sugar, water, and extract in a small bowl until smooth. Drizzle over pastries. Sprinkle with almonds. Let set 30 minutes before serving.

Crepes Suzette

Crepe Suzette is an even more avid baker than Strawberry Shortcake, which is saying something! It is their love of cooking that brings the girls together; they first met during Strawberry's trip to Pearis, and then again when Crepe visits Strawberryland (*Strawberry Shortcake: Housewarming Surprise*, 1983). Crepes Suzette is one of France's most famous desserts, consisting of thin pancakes filled with orange butter and flambéed in an orange and liqueur sauce. Its origins are disputed, but there's no question this elegant dessert will appeal to family and friends.

Serves 4

For Crepes
2 large eggs
2⅓ cups 2% milk
1 tablespoon granulated sugar
1¼ cups all-purpose flour
2 tablespoons salted butter,
   plus more for pan

For Filling
Zest of 1 large orange
6 tablespoons granulated sugar,
   divided
6 tablespoons salted butter,
   room temperature
Juice of 1 large orange

For Flambéing
¼ cup Cointreau or Armagnac
2 tablespoons brandy
1 cup sweetened whipped cream
   or vanilla ice cream

1. To make Crepes: Whisk together eggs and milk in a large bowl. Add sugar and flour and mix until smooth. Allow batter to rest 10 minutes.

2. Heat a 9" cast iron skillet or crepe pan over medium-high heat. Melt butter in pan, then whisk into batter. Pour ½ cup batter into pan and swirl until it covers bottom. Cook until batter looks dry, 2–3 minutes, then run thin spatula around edges to loosen. Ease spatula under Crepe and flip it over. Allow Crepe to cook another 30 seconds, then slide out of pan onto a large plate. Repeat with remaining batter.

3. To make Filling: Cream orange zest, 4 tablespoons sugar, and butter together in a medium bowl. Slowly mix in ½ orange juice.

4. Preheat broiler to high. Line a baking sheet with aluminum foil.

5. Spread each Crepe with 1 tablespoon orange butter, then roll into a tube. Place rolled Crepes on prepared baking sheet, making sure they are nestled close together. Sprinkle Crepes with remaining 2 tablespoons sugar, and broil 6–8 minutes until sugar is caramelized and sauce is bubbling.

6. To Flambé: Combine Cointreau, brandy, and remaining orange juice in a small saucepan. Heat over medium heat until vapor starts coming off the liquid and little bubbles form at the edges, 3–5 minutes. With a long match, carefully set mixture on fire and pour over Crepes. Once flames have gone out, serve with whipped cream or vanilla ice cream.

Gazebo-Grilled Peaches and Pound Cake

In *Strawberry Shortcake in Big Apple City* (1981), Strawberry wins the big prize in Coco Nutwork's baking contest: a gazebo! Not only is it a fun place to hang out and enjoy the garden in summer, it has a grill! The grilled peaches in this recipe go wonderfully with the vanilla pound cake. A sweet liqueur-infused cream tops the dessert for a dish that will delight whomever you invite to the summer hangout.

Serves 6

For Cake
1 cup plus 2 tablespoons cake flour
⅛ teaspoon baking powder
3 large eggs
1 cup granulated sugar
6 tablespoons cream
2 teaspoons vanilla extract
6 tablespoons salted butter, melted

For Cream
1 cup heavy cream
4 tablespoons confectioners' sugar
1½ tablespoons amaretto

For Peaches
3 large peaches, halved and pitted
2 tablespoons olive oil

1. To make Cake: Preheat oven to 325°F. Butter an 8½" × 4½" loaf pan and dust with 2 tablespoons flour.

2. Sift together remaining 1 cup flour and baking powder in a large bowl.

3. Whisk eggs in a separate large bowl on medium speed until blended. Add sugar, little by little, and keep whisking until sugar is incorporated and egg mixture is thicker and light yellow in color. Making sure not to deflate the egg mixture too much, alternately add flour mixture and cream. Stir in vanilla extract. Stir in melted butter.

4. Pour batter in loaf pan and smooth top. Bake 60–70 minutes until top is golden and a toothpick inserted in center comes out clean.

5. To make Cream: Whip cream in a chilled medium bowl until soft peaks appear. Add sugar and continue to whip until stiff peaks form. Fold in amaretto.

6. To make Peaches: Preheat grill or heat grill pan over medium heat.

7. Brush peach halves with olive oil. Grill 4–5 minutes on each side.

8. Place each Peach half on a slice of pound cake, and top with Cream. Serve.

Record-Breaking Strawberry Soufflés

One never really needs an excuse to make a soufflé, but helping a friend win something is certainly motivation! In "Berry Bitty World Record" (*Strawberry Shortcake's Berry Bitty Adventures*, Season 1, 2010), Strawberry is determined to break the record for the tallest strawberry soufflé and win a vacation for her friend Berrykin Bloom. Though they may not break a record, these little strawberry soufflés are sure to be a win with friends and family.

Makes 6 soufflés

2 tablespoons unsalted butter
¼ cup plus ⅓ cup granulated sugar, divided
2 cups hulled and sliced strawberries
½ teaspoon almond extract
⅛ teaspoon rosewater extract
4 teaspoons cornstarch
5 egg whites, room temperature

1. Preheat oven to 350°F. Grease six 1-cup ramekins with butter, then coat with 2 tablespoons sugar. Place on a baking sheet.

2. Purée strawberries, 2 tablespoons sugar, almond extract, rosewater extract, and cornstarch in a food processor.

3. Beat egg whites in a large bowl until soft peaks form. Gradually add remaining ⅓ cup sugar, beating until stiff peaks form.

4. Make an indentation in top of whipped egg whites and pour in ¼ strawberry purée. Fold purée into the whites. Keep adding purée gradually in small amounts until mixture is a light pink but still airy. Transfer mixture to ramekins.

5. Bake Soufflés 15 minutes until puffy and ever so slightly golden on edges. Garnish with sliced strawberries, if desired. Serve.

A Saucy Finish

Give these an extra pop of flavor with vanilla sauce! Whisk together 1¾ cups whole milk, 1 large egg yolk, 3 tablespoons granulated sugar, and 2 teaspoons cornstarch in a heavy-bottomed saucepan. Place over medium-low heat and, whisking constantly, cook until mixture boils and starts to thicken, about 10 minutes. Remove from heat and allow to cool for 45 minutes. Add 1 teaspoon vanilla extract. Whisk again. Cut a slit on each soufflé and pour vanilla sauce on top.

Stop-and-Go Grape Clafoutis

Sour Grapes starts out in Strawberryland as the Purple Pieman's adult sidekick, but when she's reintroduced later in "High Tech Drama" (*Strawberry Shortcake's Berry Bitty Adventures*, Season 4, 2015) she is a teenager and has a twin named Sweet Grapes. Sweet is a little bit country, while Sour is a lot rock 'n' roll. This grape clafoutis, which uses both green and red grapes, is inspired by their opposite natures, as well as their successful food truck business. Garnish with a small cluster of whole grapes for a dramatic touch.

Serves 6

1½ cups seedless green grapes
1½ cups seedless red grapes
3 large eggs
6 tablespoons whole milk
2 tablespoons orange zest
6 tablespoons granulated sugar
½ cup all-purpose flour
¼ teaspoon salt

1. Preheat oven to 350°F. Grease a 9" gratin pan or 10" porcelain tart pan with butter. Arrange grapes inside pan.

2. Whisk eggs in a large bowl until combined. Whisk in milk, orange zest, and sugar. Whisk in flour and salt, and keep whisking until batter is completely smooth.

3. Pour batter over grapes and bake 35–45 minutes until set in middle and golden. Serve warm.

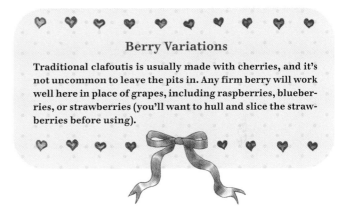

Berry Variations

Traditional clafoutis is usually made with cherries, and it's not uncommon to leave the pits in. Any firm berry will work well here in place of grapes, including raspberries, blueberries, or strawberries (you'll want to hull and slice the strawberries before using).

Chapter 3

Pies and Tarts

You would think the Peculiar Purple Pieman is the best person in Strawberryland to ask for advice on how to make a pie. But that is not the case! True, his home on Porcupine Peak is literally a stack of pie tins, and he is so dedicated to his namesake dish that he is willing to do less than berry nice things to get ingredients, but he is also usually too busy with his ongoing campaign against Strawberry Shortcake to produce a decent pie!

Luckily, this gives others a chance to shine. In this chapter, you'll find pie recipes inspired by Strawberry's friends, like Huckleberry's Pie and Honey Pie's sweet namesake. Of course, we haven't forgotten the Purple Pieman! He is the inspiration behind the strangely delicious Peculiar Purple Apple Berry Pie. And there aren't just pies included in this chapter: Don't forget to explore the tart recipes! You'll find sensational tarts worthy of Strawberryland, like Raspberry's Not-So-Tart Tarts and Apricot's Precociously Scrumptious Frangipane Tart.

Huckleberry's Pie

Huckleberry is one of the few boys in Strawberryland. He has a reputation for laziness, but is also a loyal friend. This recipe—his namesake—is a treat! Huckleberries look a lot like blueberries, but are smaller and tarter. You can use either fresh or frozen huckleberries in this pie.

Serves 8

For Crust

2½ cups all-purpose flour
½ teaspoon salt
1 tablespoon granulated sugar
1 cup (2 sticks) cold unsalted butter,
    cut into cubes
6 tablespoons ice water

For Filling

4 cups fresh or frozen
    huckleberries, thawed
Juice of 1 large lemon
½ teaspoon ground cinnamon
¼ teaspoon ground ginger
¼ teaspoon ground nutmeg
¾ cup plus 1 tablespoon
    granulated sugar, divided
2 tablespoons all-purpose flour
1 tablespoon unsalted butter,
    cut into small pieces
1 tablespoon whole milk

1. To make Crust: Add 1½ cups flour, salt, and sugar to a food processor. Pulse to combine. Arrange butter cubes over flour. Process until dough comes together.

2. Break up dough and add remaining flour. Process until dough is crumbly. Add 2 tablespoons ice water and process until a piece of dough can be pinched together without crumbling. Add more water if necessary, but no more than 6 tablespoons total, unless you live in a very dry climate.

3. Turn dough onto a floured surface and knead into a ball. Cut ball in half, wrap each half in wax paper, and refrigerate 1 hour.

4. Preheat oven to 375°F.

5. Roll out each dough half to an 11" round. Line an ungreased 9" pie pan with one Crust.

6. To make Filling: Stir together huckleberries, lemon juice, spices, ¾ cup sugar, and flour in a large bowl. Pour into lined pie pan. Dot with butter pieces.

7. Cut second Crust into strips and arrange in a lattice pattern over pie. Crimp edges. Brush crust with milk, then sprinkle with remaining 1 tablespoon sugar.

8. Bake 45–50 minutes, or until Crust is golden. Let cool 2 hours before slicing and serving.

Apricot's Precociously Scrumptious Frangipane Tart

Apricot may be one of Strawberryland's babies, but she is quite sophisticated. After all, she spent her formative years in Big Apple City's bohemian enclave, Spinach Village! This tart, therefore, offers a more worldly take on the usual stone fruit tart by combining a frangipane cream with apricot halves and an apricot glaze in a less-sweet pastry shell. Make it for your next literary salon in the city, or bring it to the next potluck. Wherever you share it, it will surely be a hit.

Serves 8

6 tablespoons unsalted butter,
    room temperature
6 tablespoons granulated sugar
2 large eggs, lightly beaten
½ cup almond flour
2 tablespoons all-purpose flour
4 teaspoons almond extract
1 (11") refrigerated piecrust
4 apricots, halved and pitted
2 tablespoons apricot jam
1 tablespoon water

1. Preheat oven to 350°F.

2. Beat together butter and sugar in a large bowl until light and fluffy. Add egg a little at a time, beating well after each addition. Stir in flours and almond extract.

3. Line a 10" tart pan with piecrust. Spread filling evenly over crust. Place apricot halves inside tart's perimeter, with one in center of filling. (You may have one half left over.)

4. Bake 35–40 minutes until filling is puffy and golden and crust is browned. Cool on rack 45–60 minutes.

5. Melt apricot jam and water in a small saucepan over low heat until smooth, about 5 minutes. With a pastry brush, paint glaze on top of tart. Serve cold or at room temperature.

A Good Time for Plums

This tart is also delicious made with pitted and halved plums. Substitute plum preserves to make the glaze.

Hard-to-Ignore Honey Pie

Honey Pie is one of the Strawberryland fillies (young female horses), and is Strawberry's own horse. Like other animals in Strawberryland, she can talk. This is not always a good thing, since she's a bit of a diva, but that doesn't stop her from being one of Strawberry's favorite companions. The classic custard pie she's named after gets some extra oomph in this recipe with a puff pastry crust, and hopefully her equine stamp of approval!

Serves 8

For Crust
1 (12") round or square sheet
    puff pastry

For Filling
4 large eggs
2½ cups whole milk
½ cup amber honey
½ cup packed dark brown sugar
½ teaspoon ground nutmeg
1 teaspoon vanilla extract
1 teaspoon almond extract
½ teaspoon salt

1. To make Crust: Preheat oven to 425°F.

2. Line a deep-dish pie pan or 8" square baking dish with puff pastry. Place a piece of nonstick aluminum foil, nonstick side down, on top of dough and fill with beans or pie weights. Bake 20 minutes. Remove foil and beans and bake 10 more minutes. Cool 10 minutes, then cover Crust edges with aluminum foil.

3. To make Filling: Reduce oven heat to 400°F. Whisk eggs in a large bowl until well blended. Whisk in milk, honey, sugar, nutmeg, extracts, and salt until well blended. Pour into Crust and bake 45 minutes, until Filling is set and a toothpick inserted in center comes out clean. Let cool 1 hour, then refrigerate 2 hours before serving.

Standing the Test of Time

Honey has been used since ancient times as a sweetener in pies. The first published pie recipe was Roman, and included goat cheese and a rye crust!

Raspberry's Not-So-Tart Tarts

Raspberry Tart has a reputation for not always being the nicest to those around her, but she has a soft spot for her best friend, Lemon Meringue. These little tarts reflect the sweeter side of her character, with a buttery crust, vanilla pastry cream, ripe berries, and a light raspberry glaze. They're also small enough to enjoy more than one! How can anyone be tart about that?

Makes 18 (2¼") tarts

For Crust
1⅔ cups all-purpose flour
¼ teaspoon salt
¼ cup unsalted butter, cubed
⅓ cup granulated sugar
1 large egg, beaten
2 teaspoons ice water

For Pastry Cream
¾ cup whole milk
2 large egg yolks
3 tablespoons granulated sugar
1 tablespoon cornstarch
1 teaspoon vanilla extract
1 pint fresh raspberries

For Glaze
4 tablespoons seedless raspberry
    preserves
2 tablespoons water

1. To make Crust: Pulse flour, salt, butter, and sugar in a food processor until butter is incorporated. Add egg and continue to pulse until a rough dough comes together. If mixture is too dry, add ice water, a few drops at a time, until dough comes together.

2. Transfer dough to a floured baking board and knead just enough to form a disk. Wrap dough in wax paper and refrigerate 1 hour.

3. To make Pastry Cream: Whisk together milk, egg yolks, sugar, and cornstarch in a small, heavy-bottomed pan. Whisking constantly over low heat, bring mixture to a boil. Keep whisking until it starts to thicken, about 10 minutes total. Remove from heat and cool completely, 45–60 minutes, before adding vanilla.

4. Preheat oven to 375°F. Roll out dough on floured surface until ⅛" thick. Line each tart pan with dough, trimming to fit. Using a fork, prick bottoms and sides of each tart.

5. Place tart pans on a baking sheet and bake until golden and slightly puffed, about 15 minutes. Allow tarts to cool 10 minutes, then remove from pans and cool 30 minutes on a wire rack.

6. Fill each cooled tart Crust with 1 tablespoon Pastry Cream and arrange raspberries on top.

7. To make Glaze: Place raspberry preserves and water in a small saucepan. Over medium-low heat, stir until preserves melt, about 5 minutes. With pastry brush, paint raspberries in tarts with Glaze (if some Glaze winds up on the Pastry Cream, that's okay). Serve.

Huckleberry Jam Crostata

For those who live in places where fresh or frozen huckleberries aren't available, this Huckleberry Jam Crostata is a great substitute for Huckleberry's Pie (see recipe in this chapter). Huckleberry jam can usually be found in specialty grocery stores or online. And since Huckleberry is a rough-and-tumble character, this rustic and unpretentious jam pie is the perfect tribute.

Serves 8

1 (11") premade piecrust
⅔ cup huckleberry jam
1 large egg, beaten
1 tablespoon water
2 tablespoons granulated sugar

1. Preheat oven to 425°F.

2. Line a baking sheet with aluminum foil or parchment paper and place crust in center of sheet.

3. Spread jam on crust, leaving a 2" border. Fold border over jam, pleating to make a circle.

4. Mix egg with water in a small bowl and brush on crust border. Sprinkle border with sugar.

5. Bake 25 minutes or until crust is golden and filling is bubbly. Serve at room temperature.

Marmalade's Fluttering Pastry Cups

Orange Blossom's pet butterfly, Marmalade, inspires these delicious little pastry cups filled with marmalade preserves. At a few bites per cup, you can't eat just one! And if marmalade is not your favorite, any other jam, jelly, or curd will do. Remember, butterflies love sugar, regardless of the flavor you choose.

Makes 24 cups

¼ cup granulated sugar
¾ cup all-purpose flour
3 tablespoons plus ½
    teaspoon cornstarch
1 teaspoon baking powder
9 tablespoons salted butter
1 teaspoon vanilla extract
½ cup marmalade

1. Preheat oven to 400°F.

2. Combine sugar, flour, cornstarch, and baking powder in the bowl of a food processor. Add butter and vanilla and process about 1 minute until dough forms.

3. Turn dough onto a floured baking board and knead into a log about 2" wide and 12" long. Slice log into twenty-four equal pieces and press each piece into an ungreased mini muffin pan cup, making sure to press dough halfway up sides. Place 1 teaspoon marmalade in each cup.

4. Bake cups 8–10 minutes until golden and puffy. Cool 15 minutes before removing from muffin pan and serving.

Peculiar Purple Apple Berry Pie

Strawberryland's villain, the Purple Pieman, can be quite peculiar. Mr. Sun certainly thinks so! Because seriously, what kind of person hates berry talk so much that he breaks down and confesses all his sins when he hears it (*Strawberry Shortcake: Pets on Parade*, 1982)? This pie dedicated to him is unusual, yes, but also quite delicious, combining apples, berries, various spices, and a purple sugar topping.

Serves 8

2 (11") premade piecrusts
1 large green apple, peeled, cored, and sliced
1 teaspoon ground cinnamon
4 tablespoons granulated sugar, divided
1 pound frozen mixed berries, thawed
2 tablespoons dark brown sugar
2 tablespoons all-purpose flour
1 teaspoon ground cardamom
1 teaspoon ground ginger
1 tablespoon crème de violette liqueur
3 drops purple food coloring
1 tablespoon water

1. Preheat oven to 425°F.

2. Line a 9" pie pan with one piecrust. Arrange apple slices on crust. Combine cinnamon and 2 tablespoons granulated sugar in a small bowl. Sprinkle over apples.

3. Combine berries, brown sugar, flour, spices, and liqueur in a large bowl. Spread over apples.

4. Top berry mixture with second crust, crimp, and trim edges. Cut an X in middle of crust.

5. Combine remaining 2 tablespoons granulated sugar and food coloring in a small bowl. Brush top crust with water and sprinkle with colored sugar.

6. Bake pie 20 minutes, then reduce heat to 350°F and bake 25 minutes or until crust is golden and sounds a bit hollow when tapped. Let pie cool 4 hours before slicing and serving.

Elusive Elixirs

Can't find crème de violette? For a slightly different floral note, use ½ teaspoon food-grade rosewater extract instead. It will be just as bizarrely intriguing!

Foreseeably Delicious Almond Tea Cakes

Almond Tea is originally from China Cup, and she and Strawberry become friends during Strawberry's around-the-world trip, taken right after the events in *Strawberry Shortcake: Pets on Parade* (1982). Almond is very sweet, a bit shy, and possibly psychic. She also has a pet panda named Marza. These delicious tea cakes inspired by her name have a rich almond filling and tender crust, and are topped with a pretty purple or yellow icing (her favorite colors).

Makes 12 tea cakes

For Dough
14 tablespoons salted butter,
   softened
⅓ cup granulated sugar
2 large egg yolks
2 cups all-purpose flour

For Filling
7 tablespoons unsalted butter,
   softened
⅓ cup granulated sugar
1½ cups almond flour
4 large eggs
2 teaspoons almond extract

For Icing
1 cup confectioners' sugar, sifted
5 teaspoons water
3 drops purple or yellow
   food coloring

1. To make Dough: Cream together butter and sugar in a large bowl until fluffy. Mix in egg yolks and flour. Wrap Dough in plastic wrap. Refrigerate 30 minutes.

2. To make Filling: Preheat oven to 425°F.

3. Stir together butter, sugar, almond flour, eggs, and almond extract in a medium bowl until smooth.

4. Divide chilled Dough into twelve equal pieces. Press each Dough piece into an ungreased cup of a cupcake or muffin tin, making sure to cover bottom and sides. Fill cups with Filling and smooth tops.

5. Bake 15 minutes until Dough is golden. Allow to cool 10 minutes, then remove cakes from tins and cool on a wire rack 30–45 minutes.

6. To make Icing: Mix sugar and water in a small bowl until a smooth paste forms. Add either purple or yellow food coloring, or divide Icing in half and use both colors. Cover top of each cake with a thin layer of Icing, making sure it doesn't drip over the sides. Let Icing set 30 minutes before serving cakes.

Baby Cherry Cribbler

Baby Cherry Cuddler first appears in *Strawberry Shortcake: Pets on Parade* (1982). Her pet is a goose named Gooseberry. Cherry isn't much of a talker, but she is quite affectionate, and eating this Baby Cherry Cribbler, with its crumbly buttery topping, tangy cherries, brown sugar, and a hint of amaretto, feels a lot like getting a hug from this sweet baby girl.

Serves 6

For Topping
1 cup all-purpose flour
6 tablespoons dark brown sugar
1 teaspoon ground cinnamon
¼ teaspoon salt
6 tablespoons unsalted butter

For Filling
1 pound fresh cherries,
    stemmed and pitted
2 tablespoons dark brown sugar
1 tablespoon all-purpose flour
1 tablespoon amaretto

1. Preheat oven to 375°F.

2. To make Topping: Mix flour, sugar, cinnamon, and salt in a medium bowl. Cut in butter until mixture resembles coarse crumbs.

3. To make Filling: Combine cherries, sugar, flour, and amaretto in a large bowl.

4. Place Filling in an ungreased 8" square baking dish and cover with Topping. Bake until Topping is browned and Filling is bubbling, about 35 minutes. Serve warm.

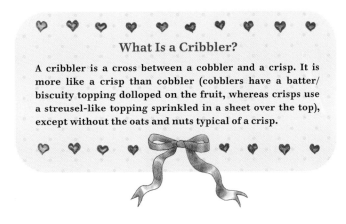

What Is a Cribbler?

A cribbler is a cross between a cobbler and a crisp. It is more like a crisp than cobbler (cobblers have a batter/biscuity topping dolloped on the fruit, whereas crisps use a streusel-like topping sprinkled in a sheet over the top), except without the oats and nuts typical of a crisp.

Worth-the-Workout Banana Cream Pie

Banana Twirl, who moves to Strawberryland right before the Berrykins reveal themselves (*Strawberry Shortcake Meets the Berrykins*, 1985), is an exercise fanatic, always looking for a chance to get her cardio on. Since she's always on the move, she can fuel up with rich desserts like this banana cream pie, full of whipped cream, vanilla pudding, and bananas on a crispy chocolate wafer crust. Surely that's the best endorsement for going to the gym!

Serves 8

For Crust
1½ cups ground chocolate wafers
4 tablespoons salted butter,
    melted
2 tablespoons granulated sugar

For Filling
2 cups vanilla pudding
2 large ripe bananas, sliced
2 cups sweetened whipped cream
2 tablespoons slivered almonds,
    toasted
1 tablespoon cocoa powder

1. To make Crust: Preheat oven to 350°F.

2. Mix wafers, melted butter, and sugar in a medium bowl. Press mixture into an ungreased heavy-duty aluminum foil–lined 9" pie pan, making sure it covers bottom and comes up sides of pan.

3. Bake 10 minutes, then cool 30 minutes.

4. To make Filling: Spread pudding on bottom of Crust. Arrange banana slices on top of pudding, then cover with whipped cream. Sprinkle almonds on top. Dust with cocoa. Refrigerate pie 1 hour before serving.

Chapter 4

Breakfast Sweets

Breakfast in Strawberryland is the most important meal of the day—after all, the Strawberryland kids need lots of energy for all that berry farming! Breakfast is also the biggest reason skillet cakes are a menu staple at the Berry Bitty Café, where proprietress Strawberry Shortcake serves her delicious creations.

In this chapter, you will discover recipes for whipping up Strawberryland-inspired breakfast treats in your own kitchen. Start the day with Berry Bitty Café's Crispy Waffles topped with whipped cream and jam. And if you're a fan of spherical pancakes, try Pupcake's Pancake Puffs. Not in the mood for pancakes or waffles? This chapter also includes muffins, coffee cakes, scones, and more—there is something for every taste! There are not-too-sweet options like Blueberry's Berry Versatile Muffins and Hopsalot's Carrot Cake Muffins. And you can satisfy a sweet tooth with baby Lem's Lemon-Lime Bundt Cake or T.N. Honey's Earl Grey Honeybee Cake. Although all the recipes in this chapter are perfect for breakfast, they are also berry much anytime treats!

Berry Bitty Café's Crispy Waffles

Waffles are a breakfast must-have at Strawberry's place of business, but these particular waffles are quite decadent, so they also qualify as dessert. Not that that is a bad thing! For some extra berry flair, try making these in a heart-shaped waffle iron and topping the jam with dollops of sweetened whipped cream.

Serves 9

1 cup (2 sticks) unsalted butter
3 large eggs
1½ cups whole milk
1 tablespoon baking powder
1 tablespoon granulated sugar
1¾ cups all-purpose flour
1 cup strawberry
    (or your favorite) jam

1. Melt butter in a medium saucepan over low heat and set aside to cool 5 minutes.

2. Whisk eggs in a large bowl until completely blended. Whisk in milk, baking powder, sugar, and flour. Whisk until well combined. Add melted butter and whisk to combine (a few lumps are okay).

3. Heat waffle iron and grease with nonstick cooking spray or vegetable oil as needed. Bake batter according to manufacturer directions. Place baked waffles in oven to keep warm while cooking the rest of the batter.

4. Serve topped with jam.

Pupcake's Pancake Puffs

Pupcake the dog is one of the three canine Strawberryland pets, and has the distinction of having had several owners throughout the series. At first, he is Huckleberry Pie's faithful companion, but in a later series he gets adopted by Strawberry ("Here Comes Pupcake," *Strawberry Shortcake*, Season 2, 2004), much to her cat Custard's dismay. These yeast-raised Pancake Puffs capture both his energy and sense of fun. Serve them dusted with confectioners' sugar, or topped with maple or fruit syrup or fruit jam.

Makes 60 puffs

1½ cups cold whole milk
2¼ teaspoons dry yeast
1¾ cups all-purpose flour
3 tablespoons granulated sugar
¼ teaspoon salt
1 large egg
3 tablespoons unsalted butter

1. In a medium saucepan, heat milk over low heat about 2 minutes or microwave about 15 seconds in a microwave-safe bowl until warm to the touch but not hot. Add yeast and stir. Set aside 10 minutes or until foamy.

2. Whisk together flour, sugar, salt, and egg in a large bowl. Whisk in milk and yeast mixture, cover bowl with plastic wrap, and set in a warm place 1 hour until doubled in volume and bubbly.

3. Place a *poffertjes*, *aebleskiver*, or *takoyaki* pan or large cast iron pan over medium heat. Coat cups (or if using cast iron pan, coat surface) with a bit of butter. Once butter has melted, fill each cup with 1 tablespoon batter. If using a cast iron pan, space out tablespoons of batter, making sure they don't touch.

4. Cook puffs until edges are almost set and bottoms are golden, 2–3 minutes. Flip puffs with a fork and cook until both sides are golden, about 3 more minutes. Remove from pan and place on a large platter. Repeat cooking with remaining batter, re-buttering cups or pan after two batches. Serve warm.

A Netherlands Treat

Dutch cooks will recognize these puffs as a version of *poffertjes*, which are similar, appearance-wise, to Danish *aebleskiver*. Where the two differ, though, is that *poffertjes* use yeast to lighten the dough instead of baking powder and baking soda.

Hopsalot's Carrot Cake Muffins

Hopsalot is Apricot's bunny companion, and is as fond of carrots as you might think. Carrots are a healthy food, packed with nutritious beta-carotene. These muffins pay tribute to Hopsalot by including carrots, but also get an extra pop of flavor from brandy-soaked raisins, and some crunch from pecans. They make a perfect breakfast, lunch, or snack.

Makes 24 muffins

¾ cup golden raisins
3 ounces brandy
Juice of 1 medium orange
1 cinnamon stick
¼ teaspoon ground nutmeg
4 tablespoons (½ stick) butter, melted
4 large eggs
¾ cup canola oil
1½ teaspoons vanilla extract
2 cups all-purpose flour
1¾ cups granulated sugar
1 teaspoon ground cinnamon
1 teaspoon ground cardamom
1 teaspoon baking powder
1 teaspoon baking soda
½ teaspoon salt
3 cups shredded carrots
1 cup chopped pecans

1. Combine raisins, brandy, orange juice, cinnamon stick, and nutmeg in a medium saucepan. Bring to a boil over high heat, then reduce to a simmer over low heat. Simmer until all liquid is absorbed, about 10 minutes, stirring occasionally. Set aside.

2. Preheat oven to 350°F. Using melted butter, grease twenty-four muffin cups.

3. Whisk together eggs, oil, and vanilla in a large bowl until slightly thickened. Add flour and sugar, ½ cup at a time, and mix. Mix in cinnamon, cardamom, baking powder, baking soda, and salt. Add carrots, pecans, and raisins. Mix until combined.

4. Fill each muffin cup halfway with batter. If there are any empty muffin cups, fill them with water. Bake 25–30 minutes or until a toothpick inserted in center comes out clean. Serve at room temperature.

Blueberry's Berry Versatile Muffins

Blueberry Muffin is Strawberry's best, most loyal friend. She is good at thinking on her feet, and can be a little shy. She loves few things more than reading (though blueberries are, of course, important to her), eventually opening her own bookstore near Strawberry's café. This muffin recipe is as subtly sweet and versatile as she is.

Makes 12 muffins

2 cups all-purpose flour
½ cup granulated sugar
1 tablespoon baking powder
1 teaspoon baking soda
¼ teaspoon salt
Zest of 1 large lemon
2 large eggs
1 cup sour cream
5 tablespoons unsalted butter,
    melted
1 teaspoon vanilla extract
1 cup fresh or frozen blueberries,
    thawed

1. Preheat oven to 375°F. Grease a twelve-cup muffin or cupcake pan with nonstick cooking spray.

2. Sift together flour, sugar, baking powder, baking soda, salt, and lemon zest in a large bowl.

3. Whisk together eggs and sour cream in a separate large bowl. Add melted butter and vanilla and stir to combine. Stir sour cream egg mixture into flour mixture until combined. Add blueberries and stir until incorporated.

4. Use an ice cream scoop to fill each muffin cup about ¾ full. Fill any unused cups with water. Bake 20–25 minutes until muffins are golden and toothpick inserted in center comes out clean.

More Muffins, Please!

For a strawberry orange variation, swap the blueberries for 1 cup chopped fresh or frozen strawberries and the lemon zest for the zest of 1 small orange. For a raspberry almond variation, swap the blueberries for 1 cup fresh or frozen raspberries, omit the lemon zest, swap the vanilla extract for almond extract, and top each muffin with 2 teaspoons slivered almonds (about a ½ cup of slivered almonds total) before baking.

Rhubarb's Raspberry Monkey Bread

Raspberry Tart's pet monkey, Rhubarb, is the inspiration behind this take on monkey bread, which is made of premade biscuit dough dredged in cinnamon and sugar, drizzled with raspberry preserves and walnuts, and baked in a Bundt pan. While no one seems to know why the treat is associated with monkeys, it's quick to put together and even quicker to pull apart and devour! Garnish with whole raspberries for a berry cute presentation.

Serves 8

½ cup granulated sugar
1 tablespoon ground cinnamon
¾ cup (1½ sticks) salted butter
1 cup raspberry preserves
2 teaspoons vanilla extract
2 (16-ounce) cans refrigerated
    biscuit dough
1½ cups walnut pieces

1. Preheat oven to 350°F. Grease a twelve-cup Bundt pan with nonstick cooking spray.

2. Stir together sugar and cinnamon in a medium shallow bowl.

3. Place butter in a microwave-safe measuring cup and microwave in 10-second increments until melted. Stir in raspberry preserves and vanilla.

4. Cut each biscuit into quarters and dredge in cinnamon-sugar mixture. Press ½ biscuit quarters into Bundt pan and sprinkle with ½ remaining cinnamon-sugar. Top with ½ raspberry mixture, then ½ walnuts. Repeat layering with remaining ingredients.

5. Bake 45–50 minutes until golden. Cool 10 minutes, then run a knife around edges of pan and remove onto a platter. Cool 30 minutes before serving.

Lem's Lemon-Lime Bundt Cake

Strawberry met British twins, Lem and Ada, in Pickle-Dilly Circus during her around-the-world trip. Little Lem and Ada later move to Strawberryland with their sheepdog, Sugar Woofer. Though he may be small, Lem is mischievous and fizzy—a lot like this Lemon-Lime Bundt Cake, which uses lemon-lime soda in its glaze to give it some big flavor. And the cake itself has plenty of lemon and lime zest, along with lemon and lime juices.

Serves 12

For Cake
2½ cups plus 2 tablespoons
    all-purpose flour
¾ cup unsalted butter,
    room temperature
1½ cups granulated sugar
3 large eggs
1 teaspoon vanilla extract
1 tablespoon lemon juice
1 tablespoon lime juice
1 cup sour cream
1 teaspoon baking soda
1 teaspoon baking powder
Zest of 1 large lime
Zest of 1 large lemon

For Glaze
3¼ cups confectioners' sugar
1 teaspoon vanilla extract
3 tablespoons lemon juice
¼ cup cold lemon-lime soda

1. To make Cake: Preheat oven to 375°F. Grease a 10" Bundt (or fluted ring) pan with butter and dust with 2 tablespoons flour.

2. In a large bowl, use an electric mixer on medium speed to beat butter and sugar until light and fluffy. Add eggs one at a time, making sure one egg is incorporated before adding another. Mix in vanilla and then lemon and lime juices. Mix in sour cream.

3. Combine remaining 2½ cups flour, baking soda, and baking powder in a medium bowl. Add flour mixture to sour cream mixture, mixing until smooth. Mix in lime and lemon zests.

4. Transfer batter to prepared Bundt pan. Smooth top of batter with a rubber spatula. Bake 40–45 minutes until a toothpick inserted in Cake comes out clean. Cool in pan 10 minutes, then invert onto a cake plate to finish cooling, 45–60 minutes.

5. To make Glaze: Sift sugar, then mix with vanilla, lemon juice, and lemon-lime soda in a medium bowl until smooth. Drizzle over cooled Cake. Slice Cake and serve.

Upside-Down Sideways Pineapple Strawberry Cake

When life hands you pineapples, make a pineapple upside-down cake! Or, in Strawberry's case, an upside-down *sideways* cake (when Berrykin Bloom fills her closet with the fruit in "Room at the Top," *Strawberry Shortcake's Berry Bitty Adventures*, Season 2, 2011). This recipe adds strawberries to her creation. Neither fruit should slide sideways too much when the results are plated.

Serves 8

For Topping
⅔ cup dark brown sugar
4 tablespoons unsalted butter
2 teaspoons vanilla extract
¼ teaspoon salt
5 canned pineapple rings
1 cup large, hulled and quartered
    fresh strawberries

For Cake
½ cup (1 stick) unsalted butter,
    room temperature
1 cup granulated sugar
2 large eggs
2 teaspoons vanilla extract
2 teaspoons baking powder
½ teaspoon salt
1⅔ cups cake flour
1 cup sour cream

1. To make Topping: Combine sugar, butter, vanilla, and salt in a small saucepan, and cook over medium heat until butter melts and mixture bubbles a bit, about 5 minutes. Pour into an ungreased 9" cake pan and tilt to make sure it coats bottom of pan. Arrange pineapple and strawberries in bottom of pan.

2. To make Cake: Preheat oven to 350°F, making sure rack is in the middle of the oven.

3. In a large bowl, use an electric mixer on medium speed to cream together butter and sugar until light and fluffy. Add eggs one at a time, mixing well to combine before adding another. Scrape down sides if necessary. Mix in vanilla, baking powder, and salt. Alternately add ⅓ cup flour and ¼ cup sour cream, ending with last ⅓ cup flour, mixing well.

4. Spread batter over fruit in pan. Smooth top of batter with a rubber spatula. Bake 35–40 minutes, until a toothpick inserted in center comes out clean and top is a light golden color.

5. Cool in pan 10 minutes, then run knife around pan edge to loosen sides. Invert Cake onto a platter. Cool 45 minutes before cutting and serving.

T.N. Honey's Earl Grey Honeybee Cake

T.N. Honey is a brainy British scientist and bee aficionada who first lives in Big Apple City, then decides to move to Strawberryland after meeting Strawberry in *Strawberry Shortcake in Big Apple City* (1981). This ring cake in her honor gets its flavor from Earl Grey, the famous bergamot-infused tea named after a nineteenth century English aristocrat, and honey, a popular sweetener for tea. It is a simply brilliant treat with either coffee or tea.

Serves 8

For Cake

1 cup cold whole milk
3 teaspoons Earl Grey tea leaves
2 cups plus 1 tablespoon all-purpose
    flour, divided
½ cup (1 stick) unsalted butter,
    room temperature
1 cup granulated sugar
2 large eggs
1 teaspoon vanilla extract
4 teaspoons baking powder

For Icing

1½ cups confectioners' sugar, sifted
1 tablespoon lemon juice
3 tablespoons water
1 tablespoon amber honey
12 sugar honeybees

1. To make Cake: Scald milk in a medium saucepan over medium heat, about 5 minutes, then add tea leaves and steep 30 minutes. Strain into a mug and set aside.

2. Preheat oven to 350°F. Grease a 9" Bundt pan with butter and dust with 1 tablespoon flour.

3. Cream butter and sugar in a large bowl. Beat in eggs one at a time. Stir in vanilla.

4. Stir together remaining 2 cups flour and baking powder in a separate medium bowl, then add to butter and sugar mixture, alternating with tea-flavored milk.

5. Scrape batter into prepared ring pan and bake 45 minutes or until a toothpick inserted in Cake comes out clean. Cool 10 minutes before inverting onto a cooling rack.

6. To make Icing: Whisk ingredients in a large measuring cup until smooth. Pour Icing over cooled Cake. Decorate with sugar honeybees.

Don't Worry, Bee Happy

You can find sugar honeybees at craft stores or online.

Mr. Wormly's Hazelnut Lingonberry Scones

Philbert Wormly III (the Berry Merry Worm) is a giant worm who provides Strawberryland's taxi service. He is a dapper sort, always impeccable in a top hat, bow tie, and perfectly folded pocket square. Hailing from Britain, he enjoys his midafternoon tea, and these Hazelnut Lingonberry Scones are the perfect pairing. Of course, they can also be enjoyed with coffee in the morning, or as a less-sweet dessert!

Makes 8 scones

½ cup dried lingonberries
1 tablespoon amber honey
½ cup whole hazelnuts
5 tablespoons salted butter
1¼ cups all-purpose flour
½ teaspoon salt
2 teaspoons baking powder
1 tablespoon granulated sugar
½ teaspoon vanilla extract
¾ cup whole milk

1. Preheat oven to 425°F.

2. Place lingonberries in a medium heatproof bowl. Add honey, then enough boiling water to cover lingonberries. Set aside.

3. Place hazelnuts in a single layer on an ungreased baking sheet. Toast until golden, about 3 minutes (watch them carefully so they don't burn). Pour toasted hazelnuts into the center of a rough towel. Rub hazelnuts until skin comes off. Transfer hazelnuts to a cutting board and chop finely.

4. Drain lingonberries.

5. In a food processor, pulse butter, flour, salt, baking powder, sugar, and vanilla until butter is incorporated.

6. Transfer to a large bowl. Stir in lingonberries and hazelnuts. Make a well in flour and nut mixture and pour in milk. Using two forks, mix to form a rough dough (do not overmix).

7. Transfer dough onto a floured surface and shape into an 8" circle. Cut circle into eight wedges and place wedges on a baking sheet greased with nonstick spray.

8. Bake 15–20 minutes or until golden. Serve warm.

Berry Swaps

Can't find lingonberries? Substitute cranberries or currants. Since currants are sweeter than lingonberries, you can skip the honey-water bath.

Chapter 5

Cookies and Bars

The wonderful thing about cookies and bars is that, unlike other desserts, they are easy to eat on the go. Such convenience is always welcome in Strawberryland, whether you're craving a quick snack between berry picking, admiring the unusually large wildlife, or looking for the energy to make a quick getaway from Porcupine Peak, lest the Purple Pieman try to snare you in one of his schemes.

The recipes in this chapter are perfect to enjoy both out and about or when spending time at home. Share Maple Stirrup Blondies with friends, keep family satisfied with Raisin Cane's Rum Raisin Cookies, or impress guests with Lemon's Fashion-Forward Meringue Squares. You may choose to serve a recipe on special occasions, like Bourbon Mint Tulip Sandwich Cookies as a celebration of spring, or Hazelnut Strawberry Valentines on Valentine's Day, to show a loved one how much you care.

Bourbon Mint Tulip Sandwich Cookies

Strawberry's international friend, Mint Tulip, may be from Hollandaise, but these cookies have an American inspiration: the mint julep, which has been the Kentucky Derby's signature cocktail since the 1930s. A cream cheese frosting, flavored with bourbon and fresh mint, is sandwiched between two sugar cookies. And to honor Mint Tulip and her love of flowers and gardening, they are shaped like tulips!

Makes 36 sandwich cookies

For Cookies
1 cup (2 sticks) unsalted butter,
    room temperature
1 cup granulated sugar
1 large egg, beaten
1 tablespoon whole milk
1 teaspoon vanilla extract
¾ teaspoon baking powder
¼ teaspoon salt
3 cups all-purpose flour
¼ cup confectioners' sugar

For Decorations
4 tablespoons whole milk
4 tablespoons pink glitter sugar
    or sprinkles
1 tablespoon green glitter sugar
    or sprinkles

For Filling
2 cups cream cheese frosting
⅓ cup finely chopped fresh mint
2 tablespoons bourbon

1. To make Cookies: Cream together butter and granulated sugar in a large bowl until pale and fluffy. Stir in egg, milk, and vanilla. Stir in baking powder and salt. Slowly add flour until dough is a bit wet but not sticky.

2. Turn dough onto a baking board lined with wax paper. Knead lightly to form a ball. Divide dough ball in half, wrap each half in wax paper, and refrigerate 2 hours.

3. Preheat oven to 375°F. Line two baking sheets with parchment paper.

4. Roll out each dough ball to ⅛" thickness, using confectioners' sugar to make sure it doesn't stick.

5. Use a tulip-shaped cookie cutter to cut seventy-two Cookies from dough and place on prepared baking sheets spaced 1" apart. Refrigerate 10 minutes.

6. To Decorate: Brush half of Cookies with milk, then sprinkle flower with pink sugar and stem with green sugar. Bake 12–15 minutes until lightly golden. Cool 5 minutes on sheets, then transfer Cookies to a cooling rack.

7. To make Filling: Mix frosting, mint, and bourbon in a medium bowl. If frosting is thin or runny, add confectioners' sugar until spreadable.

8. Match up Cookies so they align when sandwiched together. Place 1 tablespoon Filling on one bottom Cookie, top with one top Cookie, and squeeze lightly. Repeat with remaining Cookies and Filling. Refrigerate 1 hour before serving.

Can't-Stop-at-One Vanilla Butter Cookies

Butter Cookie is Strawberryland's smallest baby. She doesn't walk, she crawls, and she often gets overshadowed by louder and stronger personalities. These vanilla butter cookies are like her in that they may be unassuming at first, but once you try one of these not-too-sweet, perfectly crumbly treats, there is no way you won't crave another. And another.

Makes 42 cookies

14 tablespoons salted butter,
    cut into small pieces
2 cups plus 2 tablespoons
    all-purpose flour, divided
2 tablespoons confectioners' sugar
½ teaspoon vanilla extract
¼ cup granulated sugar

1. Preheat oven to 350°F. Line a baking sheet with parchment paper.

2. Place butter, 2 cups flour, confectioners' sugar, and vanilla in a food processor. Pulse until ingredients come together. Transfer dough to a baking board dusted with remaining 2 tablespoons flour and knead lightly to incorporate stray crumbs.

3. Form dough into a rough rectangle ½" thick. Using a fluted 1¼" cookie cutter, cut out cookies and place on prepared baking sheet 1" apart, re-forming rectangle as needed to use up all dough. (You may need to cut and bake cookies in batches.)

4. Bake 15–20 minutes until very lightly golden. Put granulated sugar in medium bowl and roll warm cookies in sugar. Serve.

A Beautiful Mold

This dough holds its shape wonderfully and works great in molds or cookie presses. Once baked, you can also dress it up with colored sugars.

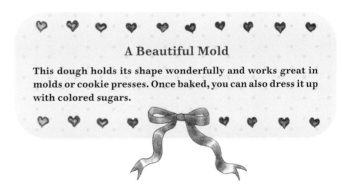

Raisin Cane's Rum Raisin Cookies

Raisin Cane is Sour Grapes's young niece, and when she comes to stay with her aunt and the Purple Pieman in Strawberryland, it's a recipe for trouble. This recipe, inspired by Ms. Cane, takes the usually staid oatmeal raisin cookie and celebrates its wild side by using rum-soaked raisins and adding toasted coconut. You may never think of the chocolate chip cookie as the more interesting one again!

Makes 24 cookies

2 cups dark raisins
¾ cup light rum
¼ cup coconut rum
2 cups shredded coconut
2½ cups steel-cut oats
1 cup (2 sticks) unsalted butter
1 cup dark brown sugar
1 cup granulated sugar
2 large eggs
1 teaspoon vanilla extract
2 cups all-purpose flour
½ teaspoon salt
1 teaspoon baking powder
1 teaspoon baking soda

1. Preheat oven to 375°F. Line two baking sheets with parchment paper or aluminum foil greased with nonstick cooking spray.

2. Place raisins, light rum, and coconut rum in a small saucepan. Bring to a boil over high heat, then reduce to a simmer over low heat. Simmer until liquid is absorbed, 15–20 minutes. Set aside.

3. Line a baking sheet with aluminum foil or parchment paper and spread coconut in a thin layer on top. Bake until coconut is golden, about 5 minutes. (Watch to make sure it doesn't burn.)

4. Place oats in a food processor and process until you have a coarse flour.

5. Cream together butter and sugars in a large bowl until fluffy. Add eggs, one at a time, mixing well after each addition. Stir in vanilla. Stir in all-purpose flour, salt, baking powder, baking soda, and oat flour. Stir in raisins and coconut.

6. Shape 2 tablespoons dough each into a ball, placing on prepared baking sheets at least 2" apart. Bake 15 minutes or until golden brown. Serve warm or at room temperature.

Maple Stirrup Blondies

After years of relying on mollusks, invertebrates, and insects to get her around town, Strawberry finally got a pony named Maple Stirrup. But this brings up a question: If a pony is the same size as a snail in Strawberryland, does that mean the pony is unusually small, or the snail unusually large? You can ponder such conundrums while having one of these blondies inspired by Maple Stirrup. They feature maple syrup instead of vanilla, and butterscotch morsels instead of chocolate ones, for a unique twist on the classic recipe.

Makes 16 bars

1 cup (2 sticks) unsalted butter,
    room temperature
1 cup lightly packed dark
    brown sugar
½ cup granulated sugar
2 teaspoons pure maple syrup
2 large eggs
1 teaspoon baking soda
1 teaspoon salt
2 cups all-purpose flour
1½ cups chopped walnuts
11 ounces (1⅛ cups) butterscotch
    morsels

1. Preheat oven to 350°F. Grease an 8" × 11" baking pan with nonstick cooking spray.

2. Cream together butter and sugars in a large bowl until fluffy. Stir in maple syrup, then eggs, one at a time, mixing well after each addition. Stir in baking soda, salt, and ½ cup of flour. Stir in remaining flour, ½ cup at a time, until it's all incorporated.

3. Fold walnuts and butterscotch morsels into batter. (Batter will be very thick.) Spread evenly into prepared pan.

4. Bake 30–35 minutes until top is golden; be careful not to overbake. Let cool completely, 45–60 minutes, before cutting and serving.

Escargot's Cookies

These delicate puff pastry cookies are dedicated to Escargot, Strawberryland's favorite snail mail carrier. While Escargot's Cookies can be filled with any sweet or savory spread, a chocolate nut spread or spicy cookie butter such as speculoos or Biscoff would surely get the snail's seal of approval.

Makes 12 cookies

2 (9¾" × 10½") sheets frozen
    puff pastry, thawed
1 cup hazelnut spread, divided
1 large egg
1 teaspoon whole milk
2 tablespoons granulated sugar

1. Roll out one puff pastry sheet on a floured surface until ⅛" thick. Spread ¾ cup hazelnut spread over it in a thin layer, then roll into a tight log. Using a serrated knife, slice log into twelve equal pieces. Place one piece cut-side down on a floured surface, cover with wax paper, and roll until doubled in size. Peel off wax paper and transfer to a large plate. Repeat with remaining pieces to create snail "shells."

2. Roll out second puff pastry sheet to ⅛" thickness. Cut into twelve strips. Spread right half of one strip with about 1 teaspoon hazelnut spread, fold left half over right half, then twist into a 4"-long corkscrew shape. Repeat with remaining strips to create snail "bodies."

3. Beat egg with milk in a small bowl. Paint each snail shell with egg wash, making sure loose end of pastry at bottom is secured. Paint each snail body with egg wash and attach to bottom of each shell, bending up along right side of shell to make the snail head and turning down on the left side of shell to make the snail tail. Refrigerate 30 minutes.

4. Preheat oven to 400°F.

5. Sprinkle snails with sugar and bake 20–25 minutes until golden. Cool 30 minutes before serving.

Lemon's Fashion-Forward Meringue Squares

Lemon Meringue is an aspiring model and fashionista, and first meets Strawberry in *Strawberry Shortcake in Big Apple City* (1981). Lemon loves nothing more than to be on trend at all times. This recipe is a fresh take on her namesake, the lemon meringue pie, that doesn't sacrifice any of the tart flavor, buttery crust, or sweet meringue topping of the original.

Makes 16

For Crust
1½ cups all-purpose flour
½ cup confectioners' sugar
¾ cup (1½ sticks) cold unsalted
    butter, cut into small pieces
1 teaspoon vanilla extract

For Filling
6 large eggs
3 cups granulated sugar
1 cup plus 2 tablespoons freshly
    squeezed lemon juice
½ cup all-purpose flour
1 teaspoon vanilla extract

For Topping
6 egg whites
1 teaspoon cream of tartar
¾ cup granulated sugar

1. To make Crust: Preheat oven to 325°F.

2. Pulse flour, sugar, butter, and vanilla in a food processor until ingredients resemble wet sand. Pat mixture into an 8" × 11" ungreased glass baking dish and bake until Crust is golden brown, 20–25 minutes.

3. To make Filling: Reduce oven temperature to 300°F.

4. Whisk together eggs and sugar in a medium bowl. Stir in lemon juice. Stir in flour and vanilla. Pour Filling in Crust and bake until Filling sets, about 40 minutes.

5. Refrigerate until fully chilled and set, 6 hours or up to overnight.

6. To make Topping: Preheat oven to 350°F.

7. Beat egg whites and cream of tartar in a large bowl on low speed until foamy. Increase speed to high and slowly add sugar; continue beating until stiff peaks form. Spread or pipe Topping over chilled Filling.

8. Bake 20–35 minutes, until meringue is golden brown and internal temperature is 160°F. Refrigerate at least 3 hours before slicing and serving.

Happily Harmonious PB&J Bars

After years of not scheming with him, snake-wielding Sour Grapes once again joins villainous forces with the Purple Pieman in *Strawberry Shortcake: Pets on Parade* (1982). While inspired by Sour Grapes and the formidable team she and the Purple Pieman make, these bars do not strike a single sour note, combining sweet and salty, smooth and crunchy, in perfect harmony.

Makes 16 bars

*½ cup (1 stick) unsalted butter,
    room temperature*
¾ cup packed dark brown sugar
¾ cup smooth peanut butter
1 large egg
1 teaspoon vanilla extract
1½ cups all-purpose flour
½ teaspoon baking powder
¾ cup grape jelly
½ cup shelled peanuts, chopped

1. Preheat oven to 350°F. Line an 8" square baking pan with wax paper.

2. Beat together butter, sugar, and peanut butter in a large bowl. Beat in egg and vanilla.

3. Stir in flour and baking powder and work it into a sticky dough. Divide dough in half and place one half in pan, flattening it and making sure it reaches corners. Remove from pan using wax paper liner, place a second piece of wax paper on top, and use a rolling pin to smooth the dough, but do not flatten it further. Freeze 10 minutes, wrapped in wax paper.

4. Line same pan with nonstick aluminum foil. Press second dough piece into pan, making sure it reaches corners. Spread jelly on top.

5. Remove first dough piece from freezer. Working quickly, unwrap from wax paper and cut into eight strips and arrange in a lattice pattern on top of jelly. Sprinkle with chopped peanuts.

6. Bake 35 minutes or until crust is golden. Cool in pan 3 hours before cutting and serving.

Nutty Alternatives

Any nut butters, chopped nuts, or jellies work in this recipe. Try almond butter with chopped almonds and raspberry jam. Or cashew butter with chopped cashews and plum jam!

Delicious-Once-You-Ditch-the-Kohlrabi Cookies

If you weren't already convinced that the Purple Pieman is peculiar, his recipe choice for the Big Apple City baking contest in *Strawberry Shortcake in Big Apple City* (1981) is kohlrabi cookies. Sure, this cabbage relative may be considered a superfood, but it is not at all suited for desserts! The sweet potato is another story: Also a superfood, it's delicious in this cookie. Spiced with nutmeg, cardamom, ginger, and cloves, and dusted with cinnamon-sugar, this goody is definitely a blue-ribbon contender.

Makes 16 cookies

1 medium sweet potato
¾ cup plus 2 tablespoons
    granulated sugar, divided
1½ cups all-purpose flour
½ teaspoon baking powder
¼ teaspoon baking soda
½ teaspoon ground ginger
½ teaspoon ground cardamom
¼ teaspoon ground nutmeg
¼ teaspoon ground cloves
¼ teaspoon salt
1 large egg
4 tablespoons unsalted butter,
    melted
1 teaspoon vanilla extract
½ cup chopped pecans
1½ teaspoons ground cinnamon

1. Preheat oven to 375°F.

2. With a fork, prick sweet potato all over, then bake on an ungreased baking sheet 1 hour or until very tender. Let cool completely, 45–60 minutes.

3. Slice potato in half and scoop flesh into a medium bowl. Mash and set aside.

4. Lower oven temperature to 350°F. Line two baking sheets with parchment paper or aluminum foil.

5. Stir together ¾ cup sugar, flour, baking powder, baking soda, ginger, cardamom, nutmeg, cloves, and salt in a large bowl. Stir in egg, butter, and vanilla.

6. Measure out ½ cup mashed sweet potato and add to dough. Fold in pecans.

7. Scoop out about 2 tablespoons of dough for each cookie, spacing them well apart on lined baking sheets. Bake 12–16 minutes until cookies look dry on top and bottoms are golden.

8. Stir together cinnamon and remaining 2 tablespoons sugar in a shallow dish. Dredge baked cookies in cinnamon-sugar mixture, then place on a rack to cool, about 15 minutes. Serve.

Cryptid Fig Bars

When Baby Needs-a-Name moves to Strawberryland in *Strawberry Shortcake and the Baby Without a Name* (1984), she doesn't find a name. But she does find a pet, a dinosaur-like creature named Fig Boot. Fig Boot is so good at hiding, leaving behind only mysterious giant footprints, that at first the kids all think he's a monster! These fig bars inspired by Fig Boot are not in the least bit monstrous, but tasty enough that they will lure any recluse out of hiding.

Makes 16 bars

For Filling
7 ounces dried figs, stemmed
1¾ cups cranberry apple juice
    cocktail
¼ teaspoon salt
Juice of ½ large lemon

For Crust
6 tablespoons unsalted butter,
    softened
¾ cup packed dark brown sugar
1 large egg
2 teaspoons vanilla extract
1¼ cups all-purpose flour
½ teaspoon baking powder
¼ teaspoon salt

Who Stepped on My Bars?

For a mysterious touch, make a footprint stencil out of cardboard, and add cocoa or confectioners' sugar Fig Boot tracks on top before cutting and serving.

1. To make Filling: Place figs, juice cocktail, and salt in a medium saucepan and cook 35 minutes over medium-low heat, stirring occasionally, until the figs are very soft. Let cool 30 minutes, then purée figs in a food processor with lemon juice.

2. To make Crust: Preheat oven to 350°F. Line 8" square baking pan with wax paper.

3. In a large bowl, use an electric mixer on medium speed to cream butter and sugar until light and fluffy. Stir in egg and vanilla. Stir in flour, baking powder, and salt. Turn dough onto a large sheet of wax paper and divide in half. Take half of dough and press into lined baking pan using a spoon lightly greased with nonstick cooking spray, making sure it completely fills the pan. Carefully lift dough sheet out of pan using wax paper, cover with another piece of wax paper, and put in freezer.

4. Line baking pan with some heavy-duty aluminum foil and press remaining dough inside, again making sure it completely fills the pan.

5. Bake dough about 20 minutes or until it just turns golden.

6. Spread Filling evenly over baked dough. Remove other sheet of dough from freezer and lay over Filling, pressing down lightly to seal. Bake 25–30 minutes until top Crust is golden brown.

7. Cool at least 1 hour. Remove from pan using foil. Peel off foil, cut into bars, and serve.

Hazelnut Strawberry Valentines

Strawberry, like many bakers, puts a lot of love into her creations. These nutty, delicate sandwich cookies (reminiscent of Linzer cookies) are filled with strawberry jam and shaped like a heart—perfect for sharing your affections in a delicious way. Who doesn't like an edible valentine any time of year?

Makes 16 sandwich cookies

10 tablespoons whole hazelnuts
½ cup (1 stick) unsalted butter,
    room temperature
⅓ cup granulated sugar
1 large egg
½ teaspoon vanilla extract
½ teaspoon baking powder
1 cup all-purpose flour
⅛ teaspoon salt
¼ cup confectioners' sugar
⅓ cup strawberry jam

1. Preheat oven to 375°F.

2. Toast hazelnuts on an aluminum foil–lined baking sheet until golden, about 10 minutes. Watch to make sure they don't burn.

3. Rub toasted hazelnuts together in a rough towel until most skins have come off. Pulse hazelnuts in a food processor until finely ground.

4. Cream together butter and granulated sugar in a large bowl. Stir in egg and vanilla, mixing well. Add baking powder, flour, ground hazelnuts, and salt, and mix until a soft dough forms. Freeze in bowl 15 minutes.

5. Turn dough out onto well-floured surface and roll to ⅛" thick. Cut out sixteen (3") hearts, then cut out a 1" heart from center of each, removing smaller hearts and adding to other dough scraps for re-rolling.

6. Place cookies on a parchment paper–lined baking sheet spaced 1" apart and bake 8–10 minutes until golden. Remove from sheet and cool on wire rack 30 minutes.

7. Roll out remaining dough and cut out sixteen more 3" hearts. Place cookies on same lined baking sheet and bake 8–10 minutes until golden. Cool on a wire rack.

8. Place cooled cutout hearts on a large sheet of wax paper. Sift confectioners' sugar on top.

9. Place 1 teaspoon strawberry jam on each whole heart, and spread to cover. Place a cutout heart on top and press down lightly. Serve.

Berry Happy Housewarming Dessert Pizzas

When bringing food to a housewarming potluck, pizza is always a great option, because it feeds many. These dessert pizzas, made with a sugar cookie crust, cream cheese frosting, and fresh berries, can also feed a crowd—like the one that helped Strawberry settle into her beautiful new home in *Strawberry Shortcake: Housewarming Surprise* (1983). Her new place may not be shaped like a shortcake, but it has far more room to entertain friends, which is a berry good thing.

Serves 16

2 pounds sugar cookie dough

2 cups cream cheese frosting

2 cups fresh raspberries,
    rinsed and patted dry

2 cups sliced fresh strawberries,
    rinsed and patted dry

2 cups fresh blackberries,
    rinsed and patted dry

2 cups fresh blueberries,
    rinsed and patted dry

1. Preheat oven to 375°F.

2. Cut dough in half and fit each half into a 12" tart pan, or roll into two (12") circles and place on aluminum foil–lined baking sheets.

3. Bake crusts 15–20 minutes or until golden. Cool 45 minutes.

4. Spread 1 cup frosting on each crust. Top with berries. Refrigerate 1 hour before slicing and serving.

Leaping Lime Bars

When not stretching at the barre or practicing her leaps, ballerina Lime Chiffon appreciates a citrusy dessert. So does her pet parrot, Parfait! You don't have to be a dancer or a bird to leap on these lime bars, though. They include key lime juice for extra tartness, a graham cracker crust, and whipped cream topping. (You can also omit the whipped cream, if preferred.)

Makes 16 bars

For Crust
3 cups graham cracker crumbs
½ cup granulated sugar
12 tablespoons (1½ sticks)
    unsalted butter, melted

For Filling
6 large eggs
3 cups granulated sugar
½ cup all-purpose flour
1 cup key lime juice
1 teaspoon vanilla extract
2 tablespoons confectioners' sugar
2 cups sweetened whipped cream

1. To make Crust: Preheat oven to 325°F.

2. Mix together graham cracker crumbs, sugar, and melted butter in a medium bowl. Pat graham cracker mixture into an 8" × 11" glass baking dish. Bake 15 minutes.

3. To make Filling: Lower oven temperature to 300°F.

4. Mix together eggs, granulated sugar, flour, lime juice, and vanilla in a large bowl until smooth. Pour Filling into Crust.

5. Bake 40–45 minutes until Filling barely jiggles. Chill at least 6 hours, preferably overnight.

6. To serve, sift confectioners' sugar over Filling. Cut and top with whipped cream.

The Tartest Treasure Hunt

If you can find the smaller, tarter key lime at your grocery store, get a few and make your own juice! Otherwise, the widely available bottled juice works just as well in this recipe.

Chapter 6

Trifles, Puddings, and Parfaits

Sometimes you're in the mood to put some effort into dessert—and sometimes you're not, particularly when temperatures rise. That's when trifles and parfaits (which call for more assembling than cooking) and puddings (which are usually light on the cooking) come in.

In this chapter, you'll find recipes for simple desserts with little or no time spent in a hot kitchen. If you're fond of trifle, the Berry Princess's Tutti-Frutti Trifle is both delicious and feeds a crowd. Or try the Berrykin Mess, which is one mess even the Princess approves of. As for parfaits, it doesn't get simpler than Plum's Perfectly Engineered Pistachio Pudding Parfaits, Parrot-Approved Citrus Chocolate Parfaits, and The Dessert That Needs a Name (feel free to name it what you like, as long as you also call it delicious!). If you don't mind using that stove or oven a bit, Custard's Strawberry Panna Cotta, Strawberry Charlotte, and Café Olé's Croissant Bread Pudding are sure to impress.

Custard's Strawberry Panna Cotta

Strawberry's pink pet cat, Custard, loves any recipe that includes cream, particularly if it also includes her human's favorite berries. In Italian, *panna cotta* means "cooked cream," but unlike many cooked puddings, it does not include cornstarch or egg yolks.

Serves 6

*¾ pound fresh strawberries,
    hulled*
2 tablespoons confectioners' sugar
½ teaspoon vanilla extract
1 cup cold whole milk
*1 tablespoon powdered
    unflavored gelatin*
1 cup whipping cream
¼ cup granulated sugar
1 teaspoon almond extract
*⅓ cup chocolate syrup or sea salt
    caramel sauce*

1. In a food processor, process strawberries with confectioners' sugar and vanilla until puréed, about 1 minute. Pour through a sieve to filter out seeds. You should have 1 cup purée.

2. Pour milk into a small bowl. Sprinkle in gelatin.

3. Pour cream and granulated sugar into a medium saucepan. Stir until sugar dissolves, then cook over medium-low heat, stirring constantly, until small bubbles form around edges, 3–5 minutes. Add gelatin milk. Continue to cook, stirring constantly, until edges bubble, 3–5 minutes.

4. Remove from heat and add purée and almond extract. Stir to combine, then pour through a sieve into a large bowl. Pour immediately into six dessert dishes or ½-cup ramekins. Refrigerate until set, 3–4 hours.

5. Serve drizzled with chocolate syrup or caramel sauce.

The More Varied, the Berrier

This recipe also works with blueberries, raspberries, or blackberries, though you may have to adjust the sugar to taste, and you may get more or less purée. If you have too much purée, serve it on top instead of the caramel or chocolate syrup.

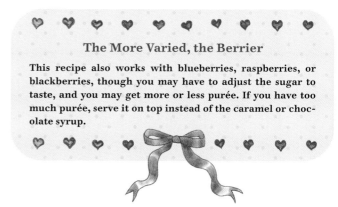

Parrot-Approved Citrus Chocolate Parfaits

Lime Chiffon's pet parrot, Parfait, is the inspiration for this elegant dessert, which layers fresh orange and grapefruit segments with a rich orange liqueur–infused pudding and lemon curd whipped cream. The word *parfait* means "perfect" in French, and the dish originated in France in the nineteenth century. While French parfaits usually include ice cream, it is not a requirement. In fact, English recipes for parfaits are closer to pâtés and are made with chicken liver!

Makes 6 parfaits

1 cup heavy cream
4 tablespoons lemon curd
2 cups chocolate pudding
2 teaspoons triple sec or Cointreau
2 large navel oranges,
    peeled and sliced
2 small ruby grapefruits,
    peeled and sliced
1 tablespoon cocoa powder

1. Whip cream in a medium chilled bowl using chilled beaters until stiff peaks form. Gently fold in lemon curd.

2. Mix pudding and liqueur in a separate medium bowl.

3. Arrange a few orange slices in each of six parfait glasses or large martini glasses. Top with pudding, then grapefruit slices. Finish with whipped cream and a dusting of cocoa. Serve.

Plum's Perfectly Engineered Pistachio Pudding Parfaits

Plum Puddin' is introduced in *The World of Strawberry Shortcake* (1980) as a brainy little boy who has a pet owl and loves to solve math problems. In *Strawberry Shortcake and the Baby Without a Name* (1984), however, Plum is a girl. This new Plum still has an owl, though, and is still very much into math and science. Plum's Perfectly Engineered Pistachio Pudding Parfaits aspire to be like one of the equations Plum is always working to balance, combining a nutty and dense pistachio pudding with fresh plums macerated in sugar and wine, chunks of pound cake, and whipped cream for a dish that equals yumminess.

Serves 4

4 large plums, pitted and sliced

2 tablespoons granulated sugar

1–2 tablespoons plum wine

2 cups pistachio pudding

2 thick slices vanilla pound cake,
    crumbled (or 20 vanilla wafers,
    crumbled)

2 cups sweetened whipped cream or
    nondairy topping

1 tablespoon chopped pistachios

1. Toss plum slices with sugar and wine in a medium bowl. Allow to sit 15 minutes to macerate.

2. In four parfait glasses (you can also use large wineglasses or martini glasses), layer pudding, macerated plums, and pound cake in two layers. Swirl on whipped cream. Sprinkle each parfait with ¼ tablespoon chopped pistachios. Serve.

Not the Season for Plums?

If fresh plums aren't in season, simply double the whipped cream amount and fold in ½ cup plum preserves and 1 table-spoon plum wine into the extra 2 cups of cream.

Berry Princess's Tutti-Frutti Trifle

As the Berrykins' ruler, the Berry Princess has a lot to manage. This trifle pays homage to her responsibilities in a tasty way by combining strawberries, blueberries, kiwifruit, bananas, and peaches with vanilla pudding, sherry-soaked ladyfingers, and whipped cream!

Serves 12

1 cup sherry
100 (4") ladyfingers
6 cups vanilla pudding (or pastry
    cream; see Raspberry's
    Not-So-Tart Tarts recipe in
    Chapter 3)
1 cup sliced fresh strawberries
1 cup fresh blueberries
1 cup sliced kiwi
1 cup sliced bananas
1 cup sliced peaches
2 cups whipped cream

1. Pour sherry into a small shallow dish. Take ladyfingers and dip them quickly (less than 2 seconds each, otherwise they will dissolve) in sherry. Dip enough of them to cover bottom of a 4-quart trifle bowl. You may have to break them to fit.

2. Cover ladyfinger layer with a layer of pudding, then top with strawberries.

3. Repeat dipping and layering ladyfingers, covering with pudding, and topping with a different fruit (remaining fruit should be used in this order: blueberries, kiwi, bananas, peaches). Top trifle with whipped cream and any remaining fruit.

4. Chill 1 hour before serving or 4 hours if you decide not to use sherry. Serve.

Expand Your Fruity Horizons

You can use all kinds of fruit in this trifle. Switch it up depending on what's in season! For a more tropical trifle, use mango and pineapple.

Café Olé's Croissant Bread Pudding

Café Olé first comes to Strawberryland to help Strawberry celebrate her new home in *Strawberry Shortcake: Housewarming Surprise* (1983). She is an artisan who loves to craft. This bread pudding in her honor, unlike most such puddings, is light and fluffy because it is made with croissants instead of denser bread. But it's still very rich, with chocolate, cinnamon, and coffee liqueur!

Serves 6

4 large plain croissants, torn
    into 1" pieces
¾ cup semisweet chocolate chips
2 large eggs, beaten
1¼ cups whole milk
¼ cup espresso or strongly
    brewed coffee
2 tablespoons Kahlúa
1 teaspoon vanilla extract
1 teaspoon ground cinnamon
3 tablespoons cocoa powder,
    divided
⅓ cup granulated sugar
¼ teaspoon salt
2 cups sweetened whipped cream

1. Preheat oven to 350°F.

2. Arrange croissant pieces in an 8" square baking pan greased with butter. Stir in chocolate chips.

3. Combine eggs with milk, espresso, Kahlúa, and vanilla in a large bowl. Whisk in cinnamon, 2 tablespoons cocoa, sugar, and salt until well combined. Pour mixture over croissants and press down with a fork to make sure they absorb liquid. Let soak 20 minutes at room temperature.

4. Bake 30–35 minutes until top looks dry and pudding is set. Slice and serve warm topped with whipped cream and dusted with remaining tablespoon of cocoa.

The Dessert That Needs a Name

Baby Needs-a-Name first comes to Strawberryland with Plum Puddin' and Peach Blush in *Strawberry Shortcake and the Baby Without a Name* (1984), and winds up with a pet, but not a name. And just like her, this dessert needs a name. Is it a parfait? Or perhaps a trifle? Either way, it is an eye-catching combination of chocolate and butterscotch puddings, layered with crushed vanilla and chocolate wafers, and topped with whipped cream.

Makes 4 parfaits

For Chocolate Pudding
2 cups whole milk
2 large egg yolks
½ cup granulated sugar
¼ cup cocoa powder
¼ teaspoon salt
2 tablespoons cornstarch
2 teaspoons vanilla extract

For Butterscotch Pudding
1½ cups whole milk
2 large egg yolks
¾ cup dark brown sugar
2 tablespoons cornstarch
¼ teaspoon salt
1 tablespoon unsalted butter
1 teaspoon whisky

For Parfaits
2 cups sweetened whipped cream
2 cups ground vanilla wafers
2 cups ground chocolate wafers

1. To make Chocolate Pudding: Place all ingredients except vanilla in a medium-sized heavy-bottomed saucepan and whisk together. Turn heat to medium and whisk constantly until mixture thickens, about 12 minutes. Set aside to cool 45 minutes, then add vanilla.

2. To make Butterscotch Pudding: Place all ingredients except butter and whisky in a medium-sized heavy-bottomed saucepan and whisk together. Turn heat to medium and whisk constantly until mixture thickens, about 12 minutes. Add butter, and stir until melted. Set aside to cool 45 minutes, then add whisky.

3. To assemble: In four parfait glasses or large wineglasses, layer whipped cream, Chocolate Pudding, vanilla wafers, Butterscotch Pudding, and chocolate wafers, finishing each with a dollop of remaining whipped cream.

Strawberry Charlotte

Different countries have their go-to strawberry desserts. Americans love strawberry shortcake. The French love *Charlotte aux fraises*, or Strawberry Charlotte, a rich yet light strawberry mousse ringed with ladyfingers. It's no coincidence then, that in France, the beloved Strawberryland resident Strawberry Shortcake bears that name! Use ribbon for an eye-catching presentation.

Serves 8

60 (4") ladyfingers
¾ pound plus 24 fresh
    strawberries, divided
⅓ cup granulated sugar
Juice of ½ large lemon
2 (0.25-ounce) envelopes
    powdered gelatin
2 cups whipping cream
2 tablespoons confectioners' sugar
½ teaspoon vanilla extract

1. Line a 9" springform pan with aluminum foil. Line bottom of pan with ladyfingers (you may have to break them to fit). To line sides, stand ladyfingers up against pan rim.

2. Purée ¾ pound hulled strawberries, granulated sugar, and lemon juice in a food processor. Pour ½ cup purée into a small microwave-safe bowl and sprinkle gelatin on top. Stir to combine.

3. Whip cream in a chilled large bowl with chilled beaters until soft peaks form. Add confectioners' sugar and vanilla and beat until peaks are stiff.

4. Microwave gelatin mixture 15 seconds or until smooth and gelatin has dissolved. Fold into whipped cream, then fold in remaining purée.

5. Pour strawberry cream into ladyfinger crust and refrigerate 4 hours up to overnight.

6. When ready to serve, garnish top with remaining 24 strawberries, whole and/or sliced, carefully remove from pan, and serve.

What's in a Name?

Strawberry's name changes country to country. In French Canada, she is called Fraisinette. In Spain, she is called Tarta de Fresa. In Mexico, her name is Rosita Fresita, and in Argentina, it is Frutillita.

Berrykin Mess

The Berrykins are funny little creatures responsible for adding scent to Strawberryland's berries. In *Strawberry Shortcake Meets the Berrykins* (1985), they get confused because of one of the Purple Pieman's cooking experiments, and suddenly everything smells off, with strawberries smelling like popcorn and raspberries like pizza. This dessert combines all kinds of different flavors, including berries, chocolate, nuts, and pretzels, and binds them together with sweetened whipped cream and crushed meringues, making for a delicious mess.

Serves 6

3 cups heavy whipping cream
3 tablespoons cream cheese
6 tablespoons confectioners' sugar
2 cups crushed meringue cookies
½ cup crushed pretzels
½ cup semisweet chocolate chips
½ cup roasted peanuts
1 cup sliced fresh strawberries
1 cup fresh blueberries
1 cup fresh raspberries

1. Whip cream and cream cheese in a large bowl until soft peaks appear. Add sugar and continue beating until stiff peaks form.

2. Transfer to an extra-large bowl and fold in remaining ingredients. Refrigerate 20 minutes, then serve in individual bowls.

I Say, That Looks Familiar!

British cooks might recognize this as a take on Eton Mess, a similar dessert served for generations at Eton, the prestigious English boys' school outside London. Eton was once attended by Prince William and Prince Harry.

Chapter 7

Ice Creams, Frappés, and Drinks

When summertime hits Strawberryland, the living is easy—particularly when there are plenty of cold things to eat and drink. But that doesn't mean Strawberry and her friends only enjoy such treats during the warmer months, and you shouldn't either!

In this chapter, you will find recipes to refresh you throughout the year, whether you're having a Snail Cart Picnic Strawberry Ice Cream Sundae, a Gazebo-Grilled Banana Split in the backyard to celebrate the end of summer, or one of Sugar Woofer's Ice Cream Sandwiches when you're cozy and warm indoors. Also, Ada recommends you try her Lemon Drop Granita, which is just smashing. Otherwise, Café Olé will be thrilled if you make one of Mexicocoa's Cinnamon Chili Frozen Hot Chocolates, as will Strawberry if you sample one of her Berry Bitty Café Rainbow Shakes. Or try Citrusy Friendship Meringue Ice Cream Oranges in honor of Lemon Meringue and Orange Blossom. And rest assured that Blueberry Muffin's Berry Scary Blueberry Milkshakes are not alarming, but delicious.

111

Berry Bitty Café Rainbow Shake

Strawberry is all about her favorite berries, of course, but the signature drink at her place of business—the Rainbow Shake—mixes things up a bit, both color- and flavor-wise. This recipe is a simplified take on hers, and is just as tasty (and pretty to look at!).

Serves 1

2 cups vanilla ice cream
¼ cup 2% milk
1 tablespoon vanilla
    simple syrup
1 teaspoon vanilla extract
3 drops each red, orange,
    yellow, green, blue, and
    purple food coloring
½ cup whipped cream
1 teaspoon rainbow sprinkles

1. Freeze a 16-ounce glass and six small bowls 15 minutes.

2. Blend ice cream, milk, syrup, and extract in a blender until very thick and completely smooth.

3. Divide ice cream blend among chilled bowls and, working quickly, mix one food coloring into each bowl. Pour red mixture into chilled glass. Place glass and remaining bowls in freezer 15 minutes.

4. Layer remaining colors, stirring each in bowl first in case it has gotten too solid, in glass. Top glass with whipped cream and sprinkles. Serve immediately.

Snail Cart Picnic Strawberry Ice Cream Sundaes

While Escargot is mostly known for delivering Strawberryland's mail *veeery* slowly, he can sometimes be persuaded to let the Strawberry kids hitch him to a cart and take them to the park. While most people won't have access to his services, there's no reason not to go to the park when you can! Pack a cooler (strawberry-shaped if you have it) with everything needed for these delicious sundaes, which combine ice cream, strawberries, pound cake, and whipped cream for an irresistible alfresco treat.

Serves 4

2 cups sliced fresh strawberries

Juice of 1 lemon

2 tablespoons granulated sugar

1 cup vanilla ice cream

4 slices vanilla pound cake,
*   crumbled*

1 cup strawberry ice cream

2 cups sweetened whipped cream
*   or nondairy topping*

1. Stir together strawberries, lemon juice, and sugar in a medium bowl and let sit 10 minutes to macerate.

2. In four sundae glasses or ice cream bowls, layer vanilla ice cream, pound cake, strawberries, and strawberry ice cream until you almost reach the top. Top with whipped cream. Enjoy immediately.

I Scream for Homemade Ice Cream

Is your ice cream maker gathering dust in a kitchen cabinet? Use the easy strawberry ice cream recipe in the Gazebo-Grilled Banana Splits (see recipe in this chapter) in place of store-bought.

Ada's Lemon Drop Granita

Ada, one of the Pickle-Dilly Circus twins, enjoys mischief as much as her brother, Lem. Lemon drops are a classic British sweet, and their intense citrus flavor translates well into this frozen treat, which is easy to prepare and doesn't require an ice cream maker.

Makes 1¼ pints

2 cups water
1 cup granulated sugar
¾ cup lemon juice
2 cups whipped cream

1. Place water and sugar in a medium saucepan and stir over high heat until sugar has dissolved. Bring to a boil and boil 5 minutes.

2. Cool syrup to room temperature, 45–60 minutes, then add lemon juice. Pour into an 8½" × 4½" loaf pan and freeze 30 minutes.

3. Scrape any ice crystals that have formed on sides into pan. Continue freezing and scraping crystals at 30-minute intervals until mixture is completely frozen and looks like fluffy, slightly wet snow, 4–6 hours.

4. Scoop into bowls and serve topped with whipped cream.

More Icy Goodness

To make orange granita, use 2 cups of water and ¾ cup of sugar for the syrup, and 1 cup orange juice and juice of 1 lemon. To make strawberry granita, use 1 cup of water and ½ cup of sugar for the syrup, and 2 tablespoons lemon juice and 2 cups whole strawberries, puréed.

Berry Scary Blueberry Milkshakes

Sometimes when you stare into the blueberry abyss, it stares back at you. At least, that's the lesson Strawberry and her friends learn when Huckleberry Pie persuades them to explore a house that may or may not be haunted by the Blueberry Beast ("The Blueberry Beast," *Strawberry Shortcake*, Season 2, 2005). Inspired by the Blueberry Beast, this milkshake not only tastes great, but will literally keep an eye on you as you drink it!

Serves 2

For Decoration
4 regular marshmallows
4 fresh blueberries

For Milkshakes
2 cups frozen blueberries
2 cups vanilla ice cream
2 cups 2% milk
2 tablespoons blueberry
*   simple syrup*

1. To make Decoration: Hollow out a small piece of the center of one flat side of each marshmallow. Press fresh blueberry into each hollowed space, making sure stem side is facing out. Secure 2 blueberry marshmallows together using two toothpicks through the rounded sides, leaving exposed toothpick on the side as anchor for glass.

2. To make Milkshakes: Blend frozen blueberries, ice cream, milk, and syrup in a blender until smooth. Pour into two large milkshake glasses and set a pair of marshmallow eyes on top of each shake. Serve.

Citrusy Friendship Meringue Ice Cream Oranges

Lemon Meringue and Orange Blossom are longtime friends, first in Big Apple City and then in Strawberryland. Both girls have an appreciation for beauty, since Orange is an artist, and Lemon loves fashion. This recipe for oranges stuffed with ice cream, topped with Swiss meringue, then baked until the meringue is golden celebrates their sweet and citrusy connection in a most delicious and eye-catching way.

Serves 8

4 large oranges, halved
1 pint orange sherbet
1 pint vanilla ice cream
6 egg whites
9 tablespoons granulated sugar
⅜ teaspoon cream of tartar

1. Juice oranges. (Use juice for other purpose or discard.) Place orange halves on a baking sheet. If they won't stay flat, trim a little off the bottoms. Fill each orange half with orange sherbet, then vanilla ice cream. Smooth tops, wrap in plastic wrap, and freeze until solid, at least 6 hours up to overnight.

2. Stir egg whites, sugar, and cream of tartar in a medium heatproof bowl. Place bowl over a barely simmering pot of water, making sure bowl's bottom isn't immersed. Stir constantly until mixture reaches 160°F on a candy thermometer, about 20 minutes.

3. Remove bowl from water bath and beat whites until glossy and can hold an almost stiff peak.

4. Preheat broiler to high.

5. Cover each frozen filled orange half with a layer of meringue. Broil orange cups 5 minutes or until meringue is golden. Serve immediately.

Any Citrus Will Do

You also can make this recipe with lemon or grapefruit cups and any combination of ice cream and sorbet or sherbet flavors.

Zesty Lemon Frappés

While the word *frappé* is French, and comes from the verb *frapper*, "to hit or beat," the popular café frappé was invented by a Greek Nestlé employee in the 1950s, and is the national coffee beverage of Greece. But frappés don't always have to be made with coffee. Try this easy and tasty recipe inspired by Lemon Meringue's pet frog, Frappé. It combines lemon simple syrup with ice cream and soda, and is a perfect refresher on a hot day.

Serves 2

6 tablespoons lemon
    simple syrup
¼ cup cold water
1 cup vanilla ice cream
6 ounces ginger ale

1. Blend syrup, water, and ice cream together in a blender until smooth.

2. Divide mixture among two tall glasses, then pour ginger ale into each glass (be careful, to avoid it fizzing over the top). Stir and serve.

A Fizz with a Jolt

Want a spicier drink? Substitute ginger beer (the pepperier the better) for the ginger ale!

Mexicocoa's Cinnamon Chili Frozen Hot Chocolates

Before Café Olé moved to Strawberryland, she lived in Mexicocoa, where they enjoy their hot chocolate mixed with cinnamon and a dash of chili. The word *chocolate* comes from the Nahuatl word *xocolatl*, or "bitter water," but there's nothing bitter about this recipe, which combines hot and cold, and spicy and sweet, in a most delightful way.

Serves 2

3 ounces bittersweet chocolate,
  finely chopped
2 tablespoons plus 1 teaspoon
  cocoa powder, divided
3 tablespoons granulated sugar
1 teaspoon ground cinnamon
1 teaspoon vanilla extract
¼ teaspoon chili powder
¼ cup heavy cream
¾ cup whole milk
2 cups crushed ice
½ cup sweetened whipped cream

1. Melt chocolate in a medium heatproof bowl over a water bath or in microwave in 15-second increments, stirring after each heating. Stir in 2 tablespoons cocoa, sugar, cinnamon, vanilla, chili powder, and heavy cream until smooth.

2. Place milk, ice, and chocolate mixture in a blender and blend until smooth. Divide among two glasses, top with whipped cream, and dust with remaining teaspoon cocoa. Serve.

Feeling Hot, Hot, Hot?

Chili powder isn't quite as spicy as cayenne powder, so if you like more of a kick to your drink, substitute cayenne powder to taste.

Sugar Woofer's Ice Cream Sandwiches

Sugar Woofer belongs to Lem and Ada, the Pickle-Dilly Circus twins, and is one of three canine pets in Strawberryland. A big, fluffy sheepdog, he is the inspiration behind these big, fluffy Ice Cream Sandwiches. Made with vanilla wafers and vanilla ice cream, they are great any time of year, for any occasion.

Serves 8

For Wafers
½ cup (1 stick) unsalted butter, room temperature
1 cup granulated sugar
1 large egg
2 teaspoons vanilla extract
1⅓ cups all-purpose flour
¾ teaspoon baking powder
¼ teaspoon salt

For Ice Cream
1½ cups heavy cream
1½ cups 2% milk
¾ cup granulated sugar
2 teaspoons vanilla extract
1 cup rainbow sprinkles

1. To make Wafers: Preheat oven to 350°F. Line two baking sheets with aluminum foil or parchment paper.

2. Cream together butter and sugar in a large bowl until fluffy. Stir in egg and vanilla. Add flour, baking powder, and salt, stirring until smooth dough forms.

3. Divide dough into sixteen balls, and place well apart on baking sheets, eight to each sheet. Bake 15–17 minutes until golden. Cool on a wire rack 30 minutes.

4. To make Ice Cream: Whisk together cream, milk, sugar, and vanilla in a large bowl until sugar is dissolved. Chill 4–6 hours until completely cold, then churn in an ice cream maker according to manufacturer's directions.

5. To assemble: Pile flat side of eight Wafers with 3 heaping tablespoons Ice Cream each. Top with remaining Wafers, flat-side down, pressing lightly to sandwich together. Wrap sandwiches in plastic wrap and freeze 2 hours to set. Before serving, let sandwiches thaw 5 minutes, then roll Ice Cream sides in rainbow sprinkles.

Cookie Swap

The ice cream in this recipe works well with any kind of cookie. Consider trying it with Raisin Cane's Rum Raisin Cookies or Delicious-Once-You-Ditch-the-Kohlrabi Cookies (see recipes in Chapter 5).

Gazebo-Grilled Banana Splits

Strawberry loves entertaining her friends at her gazebo garden house, particularly since it has a grill. And grills aren't just for savory foods! They also work for delicious desserts, like this banana split made with grilled cinnamon-sugar bananas topped with chocolate syrup, condensed milk, strawberry ice cream, roasted peanuts, and whipped cream.

Serves 2

For Ice Cream
1 pound fresh strawberries, hulled
1 cup plus 2 tablespoons
*   confectioners' sugar, sifted*
1 cup heavy whipping cream

For Bananas
1 tablespoon granulated sugar
1 teaspoon ground cinnamon
2 large just-ripe bananas,
*   unpeeled, halved horizontally*
1 tablespoon canola oil

For Topping
4 tablespoons chocolate syrup
4 tablespoons sweetened
*   condensed milk*
¼ cup roasted peanuts, chopped
1 cup whipped cream

1. To make Ice Cream: Purée strawberries with sugar in a food processor.

2. Using a chilled bowl and beaters, whip cream to stiff peaks. Fold in strawberry purée. Chill purée mixture at least 6 hours up to overnight.

3. Churn in an ice cream maker according to manufacturer's directions.

4. To make Bananas: Heat charcoal grill, gas grill, or grill pan over high heat.

5. Combine sugar and cinnamon in a small bowl. Brush Bananas with canola oil, then sprinkle with cinnamon-sugar.

6. Grill Bananas, cut-side down, 3 minutes. Flip and grill 5 more minutes.

7. To assemble: Peel Bananas, cut in half crosswise, then place four quarters each in two ice cream bowls. Drizzle with chocolate syrup and condensed milk and top with peanuts, a generous scoop of Ice Cream, and whipped cream. Serve.

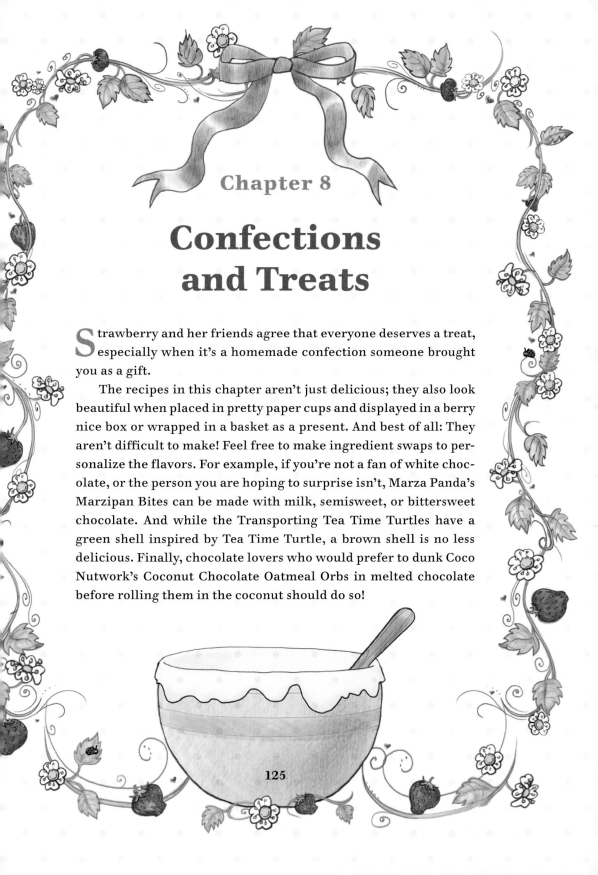

Chapter 8

Confections and Treats

Strawberry and her friends agree that everyone deserves a treat, especially when it's a homemade confection someone brought you as a gift.

The recipes in this chapter aren't just delicious; they also look beautiful when placed in pretty paper cups and displayed in a berry nice box or wrapped in a basket as a present. And best of all: They aren't difficult to make! Feel free to make ingredient swaps to personalize the flavors. For example, if you're not a fan of white chocolate, or the person you are hoping to surprise isn't, Marza Panda's Marzipan Bites can be made with milk, semisweet, or bittersweet chocolate. And while the Transporting Tea Time Turtles have a green shell inspired by Tea Time Turtle, a brown shell is no less delicious. Finally, chocolate lovers who would prefer to dunk Coco Nutwork's Coconut Chocolate Oatmeal Orbs in melted chocolate before rolling them in the coconut should do so!

Crispy Marshmallow Lucky Bugs

Ladybugs are often a great help in the garden, keeping plants free of pesky aphids. In Strawberryland, a ladybug named Lucky Bug is not just helpful; she's also a devoted friend to Strawberry and the rest of the kids, and plays an important part in Strawberry's birthday celebration in *The World of Strawberry Shortcake* (1980). These tasty marshmallow puffed rice creations are shaped in her honor, and decorated with fondant in a classic ladybug pattern.

Makes 12 ladybugs

For Lucky Bugs
6 cups puffed rice cereal
3 tablespoons unsalted butter
1 (12-ounce) package regular
    marshmallows
6 drops red food coloring

For Decoration
8 ounces semisweet chocolate,
    finely chopped
1 (4.4-ounce) package
    vanilla fondant
1 (4.4-ounce) package
    chocolate fondant

Prefer Yellow Ladybugs?

Use yellow food coloring in the marshmallow coating for a sunny Lucky Bug. You can also use melted white chocolate to dip the head of the Lucky Bug.

1. To make Lucky Bugs: Pour cereal into a large bowl.

2. Melt butter in a nonstick skillet over medium-low heat. Add marshmallows and heat, stirring constantly, until they are melted and smooth, about 5 minutes. Stir in food coloring.

3. Pour marshmallow mixture over cereal and stir until it is completely coated. Press mixture into 3" oval silicone baking molds or plastic Easter egg halves well-greased with nonstick cooking spray. Remove from molds and place on a baking sheet lined with aluminum foil or parchment paper.

4. To make Decoration: Melt chocolate in a medium heatproof bowl over a water bath or in a microwave in 10-second increments. Dip one end of each cereal oval in chocolate, covering ¼ of body. Place back on baking sheet.

5. Roll vanilla fondant into twenty-four balls, each the size of ¼" pea. Flatten each ball and top with a flattened ball of chocolate fondant the size of a chia seed to create twenty-four eyes.

6. Roll some chocolate fondant into twelve fat 1"-long strings. Cut each string in half and shape into antennae that are thick on the bottom and tapered on top. Roll more chocolate fondant into sixty pea-sized balls. Flatten balls.

7. Place two fondant eyes on chocolate-dipped part of each cereal oval and stick antennae above eyes. Place five chocolate fondant dots across each Lucky Bug. Serve.

Coco Nutwork's Coconut Chocolate Oatmeal Orbs

Coco Nutwork is the man in charge of the TV studio where Strawberry and the Purple Pieman compete to see who the best baker in Strawberryland is (*Strawberry Shortcake in Big Apple City*, 1981). Although Mr. Nutwork is hypnotized and makes the bad judgment of awarding first place to the Pieman's hideous kohlrabi cookies, he realizes his mistake. Fortunately, these simply scrumptious Coconut Chocolate Oatmeal Orbs inspired by his name will never be a mistake. Present these in cupcake liners for a berry cute touch.

Makes 12 orbs

1½ cups steel-cut oats
½ cup granulated sugar
3 tablespoons cocoa powder
⅛ teaspoon salt
10 tablespoons unsalted butter,
    room temperature
2 tablespoons espresso or
    strongly brewed coffee
1 teaspoon vanilla extract
1 cup shredded coconut

1. Pulse oats, sugar, cocoa, and salt in a food processor until finely ground. Add butter, espresso, and vanilla and process until smooth. Scrape mixture into a large bowl and refrigerate 1 hour.

2. Pour coconut onto a small plate or in a shallow dish. Line a platter with wax paper. Scoop out 2 tablespoons chilled oatmeal mixture, roll into a ball, coat in coconut, and place on wax paper. Repeat with remaining oatmeal mixture. Refrigerate 3 hours before serving.

Sometimes You Feel Like a Coconut...

Not in a coconut mood? Try rolling these orbs in chopped peanuts, walnuts, or pecans instead. You can also roll them in sprinkles or pearl sugar.

Transporting Tea Time Turtles

Apple Dumplin's pet turtle, Tea Time, gets an edible tribute with these fun chocolate, pecan, and caramel confections. You don't have to dye the chocolate shell green if you don't want to, but it is a nice homage to Tea Time. After all, it takes a bit of effort for her to carry Apple around on her back all day!

Makes 24 turtles

120 pecan halves
30 caramels, unwrapped
3½ tablespoons heavy cream
12 ounces white chocolate,
    finely chopped
1 teaspoon vanilla extract
3 drops green food coloring
2 drops yellow food coloring

1. Line two baking sheets with nonstick aluminum foil.

2. Arrange five pecans in a five-point-star shape on foil. Repeat with more pecans, leaving space between each, until baking sheets are full.

3. Place caramels and cream in a medium nonstick saucepan and heat over medium heat, stirring frequently, until caramels melt and combine smoothly with cream, about 5 minutes. Spoon a tablespoon of caramel on each pecan star. Allow to set 10 minutes.

4. In medium microwave-safe bowl, microwave chocolate in 15-second increments, stirring in between. As chocolate starts melting, reduce heating time to 10 seconds. When almost all the chocolate has melted, remove from microwave and stir until smooth. Stir in vanilla. Place ¼ chocolate in a separate medium bowl. Dye ¾ melted chocolate green and remaining ¼ chocolate yellow.

5. Cover each caramel with 1 tablespoon green chocolate. Smooth out green chocolate, then dot with ½ teaspoon yellow chocolate. Let turtles set 2 hours before serving.

Want More Flavor?

Toast pecans in a 375°F oven for 3–5 minutes until golden. Keep a close watch so they don't burn! Once they are cool, about 20 minutes, use in the recipe.

Marza Panda's Marzipan Bites

Marza Panda is Almond Tea's loyal pet bear, and possibly as psychic as she is. But you don't need a sixth sense to enjoy these white chocolate–dipped marzipan treats! You also don't have to make your own marzipan; you can buy it. Just make sure it's labeled as "marzipan," not "almond paste." Not sure about the difference between marzipan and almond paste? Marzipan includes a hint of rosewater extract, which gives it a wonderful depth of flavor.

Makes 14 bites

For Marzipan

1½ cups plus 2 tablespoons
    confectioners' sugar, divided
1½ cups almond flour
2 teaspoons almond extract
½ teaspoon rosewater extract
1 large egg white

For Couverture

16 ounces white chocolate,
    chopped
3 drops purple food coloring

1. To make Marzipan: Dust a large cutting board with 2 tablespoons sugar. Pulse flour, remaining 1½ cups sugar, extracts, and egg white in a food processor until they come together. Transfer to cutting board and knead into a ball, incorporating any crumbly parts. Cover tightly in wax paper so it won't dry out before using.

2. Line a small tray or platter with wax paper. Roll Marzipan into fourteen balls and place on tray. Line a baking sheet with wax paper. Set aside.

3. To make Couverture: Microwave white chocolate in a large microwave-safe bowl on high in 15-second increments, stirring in between. As chocolate starts melting, reduce heating time to 10 seconds. When almost all chocolate has melted, remove bowl from microwave and stir until smooth. Add food coloring and mix until combined.

4. Using a slotted spoon, coat each Marzipan ball in chocolate and place on prepared baking sheet, making sure to leave space between balls. Allow chocolate to set 2 hours at room temperature before serving.

Concerned about Raw Egg Whites?

You can substitute with pasteurized egg whites if preferred. If using egg whites from a carton, 3 tablespoons of the substitute is equivalent to 1 large egg white.

US/Metric Conversion Chart

VOLUME CONVERSIONS

US Volume Measure	Metric Equivalent
⅛ teaspoon	0.5 milliliter
¼ teaspoon	1 milliliter
½ teaspoon	2 milliliters
1 teaspoon	5 milliliters
½ tablespoon	7 milliliters
1 tablespoon (3 teaspoons)	15 milliliters
2 tablespoons (1 fluid ounce)	30 milliliters
¼ cup (4 tablespoons)	60 milliliters
⅓ cup	90 milliliters
½ cup (4 fluid ounces)	125 milliliters
⅔ cup	160 milliliters
¾ cup (6 fluid ounces)	180 milliliters
1 cup (16 tablespoons)	250 milliliters
1 pint (2 cups)	500 milliliters
1 quart (4 cups)	1 liter (about)

WEIGHT CONVERSIONS

US Weight Measure	Metric Equivalent
½ ounce	15 grams
1 ounce	30 grams
2 ounces	60 grams
3 ounces	85 grams
¼ pound (4 ounces)	115 grams
½ pound (8 ounces)	225 grams
¾ pound (12 ounces)	340 grams
1 pound (16 ounces)	454 grams

OVEN TEMPERATURE CONVERSIONS

Degrees Fahrenheit	Degrees Celsius
200 degrees F	95 degrees C
250 degrees F	120 degrees C
275 degrees F	135 degrees C
300 degrees F	150 degrees C
325 degrees F	160 degrees C
350 degrees F	180 degrees C
375 degrees F	190 degrees C
400 degrees F	205 degrees C
425 degrees F	220 degrees C
450 degrees F	230 degrees C

BAKING PAN SIZES

American	Metric
8 x 1½ inch round baking pan	20 x 4 cm cake tin
9 x 1½ inch round baking pan	23 x 3.5 cm cake tin
11 x 7 x 1½ inch baking pan	28 x 18 x 4 cm baking tin
13 x 9 x 2 inch baking pan	30 x 20 x 5 cm baking tin
2 quart rectangular baking dish	30 x 20 x 3 cm baking tin
15 x 10 x 2 inch baking pan	30 x 25 x 2 cm baking tin (Swiss roll tin)
9 inch pie plate	22 x 4 or 23 x 4 cm pie plate
7 or 8 inch springform pan	18 or 20 cm springform or loose bottom cake tin
9 x 5 x 3 inch loaf pan	23 x 13 x 7 cm or 2 lb narrow loaf or pate tin
1½ quart casserole	1.5 liter casserole
2 quart casserole	2 liter casserole

Index

About the Author

A.K. Whitney is a Los Angeles–based journalist with almost three decades of experience in print and online publications, including seven years as the food section editor at the *Press-Telegram* in Long Beach, California, and seven years as a food columnist for the Southern California News Group. Born in Sweden, she lived in Scotland, Italy, and Mexico before moving to the United States at age fifteen. She has a bachelor's degree in English literature from Bryn Mawr College, and a master's degree from the Annenberg School of Journalism at the University of Southern California. She fell in love with baking when she got her first Easy-Bake Oven (a red Italian version) at age five. She fell in love with Strawberry Shortcake at age ten, while on vacation in southern France.

BRING THE THRILL OF UNIVERSAL STRAIGHT TO YOUR KITCHEN!

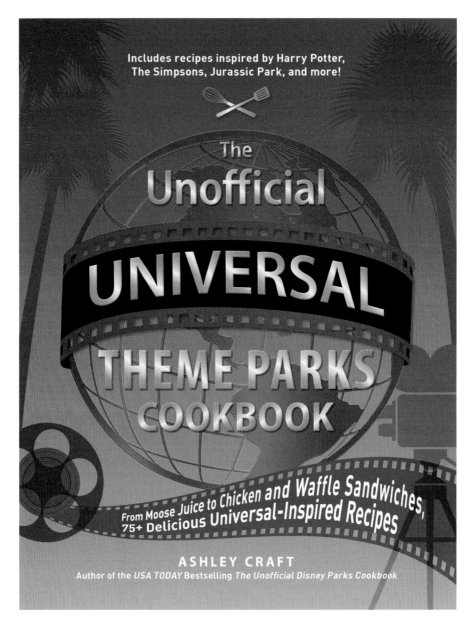

Pick Up or Download Your Copy Today!